MW00441163

FREE GAME

A Parents' Guide to Navigating Black/Brown Children Through Youth Sports and Beyond

Khalid Diallo Akhdaru Green

Copyright © 2022 by Khalid Diallo Akhdaru Green

All rights reserved. No part of this publication may be reproduced, distributed, or transmitted in any form or by any means, including photocopying, recording or other electronic or mechanical methods, without the prior written permission of the author, except in the case of brief quotations embodied in reviews and certain other non-commercial uses permitted by copyright law.

Printed in the United States of America
ISBN: 978-1-956019-39-1 (paperback)
ISBN: 978-1-956019-40-7 (ebook)

Canoe Tree
Press

4697 Main Street
Manchester Center, VT 05255

Canoe Tree Press is a division of DartFrog Books.

ADVANCED PRAISE FOR *FREE GAME*

"*Free Game* brings to bear the wide range of challenges often confronted by Black and Brown parents and student-athletes. Khalid challenges our children to see themselves from a holistic perspective rather than the limited view of the shallow athlete. What's more, he encourages our youth to boldly learn from the lessons of their sport forebears whose shoulders on which they stand, such as myself along with Muhammad Ali, Curt Flood, Connie Hawkins, Pee Wee Kirkland, and many others that have made the sacrifice so that equity and justice for our people could be achieved. More importantly, Mr. Green bravely confronts the structural anti-black racism that he has encountered and witnessed within education as well as athletics. Khalid Green has dedicated his life as a coach, mentor, NBA scout, and college professor. The mental seeds that he plants in this publication are his testimonial. *Free Game* serves as the ultimate GPS tracking system that will help parents navigate the student-athlete journey."

—Dr. John Carlos

"Khalid knows hoop on all levels. The Morehouse man spent over 10 years as an NBA scout. He is also well respected in the AAU basketball world and as a high school coach. There isn't a level of basketball he has not touched. With that in mind, Khalid's book Free Game is worth any basketball lover's time."

—Marc J. Spears, senior NBA writer for ESPN's *The Undefeated*, and author of *The Spencer Haywood Rule: Basketball, Battles, and the Making of an American Iconoclast*

"Khalid Green has been my mentor since he coached me as a 14-year-old young man. His advice, [counsel] and guidance has made a tremendous impact on my career. *Free Game* is a must read and I highly recommend it to all players, coaches and parents in the complicated sports industry."

—Kyle Neptune, head men's basketball coach, Villanova University

"I have known Khalid for over 20 years. He was my assistant coach with the Long Island/NY Panthers Basketball Grassroot program. His keen eye for talent helped identif[y] Lance Stephenson (NBA Pro), Sylven Landesburg (ACC Freshman of the Year and Overseas Pro), Devin [Ebanks] (NBA, Overseas), etc. at a young age. His personality and charisma have a warming effect, not only with players, but their parents. He is like a younger brother who is always there when I need him. The fact that he was the head coach at powerful Bishop Loughlin High School, NBA Scout, mentor to many players (including head coach at Villanova, Kyle Neptune) has only enhanced his status in the game of basketball. His book is a must read for all parents and players who want to understand how to navigate the world of youth basketball."

—Gary Charles, founder of ABIS

ACKNOWLEDGMENTS

The game of basketball has taken me places and allowed me to meet people I could have never imagined. I owe a debt of gratitude to the game and to those who laid the foundation before me.

Sharing my experiences in a book has always been my dream and vision, and my mother, Marguerite Mariama, originally planted the seed of that vision. She raised me to be a fearless black man who could aspire to be whomever I dreamed of being in life. She is the reason I have always enjoyed reading and writing. In my darkest hours, my mother was the only light I saw.

My father, Roger Green, played a pivotal role in my life also by helping me harness my vision of starting my own AAU basketball program. He helped me raise resources, creating long-lasting memories for the youth who played for me and giving life-changing opportunities, including their first trips on planes, a platform to gain college scholarships, the opportunity to develop lifelong friendships, as well as career opportunities. We named that program Brooklyn Bridge Basketball.

I am grateful also to my stepdad, Ralph Moore, who nudged, motivated, and implored me to put my depth of basketball experiences on paper to share.

I would like to thank my beautiful fiancée, Najuma, whose patience is priceless. Thank you for your emotional support while I wrote this book. You are my heart and my Earth.

I thank my young, beautiful sister, Imani, who has inspired me to be even more of a "go-getter."

I would like to thank my "sister" Chalet for motivating me to write this book. Your two books were a huge source for the completion of this one.

And I want to thank Coach Ray Haskins of Long Island University, who gave me my first opportunity to learn from a front row view what it means to be a master coach. Two years serving as your Graduate Assistant was priceless.

Shout out to Dwayne "Tiny" Morton for our run with Juice All-Stars and the historic year I was your assistant coach at Lincoln High School where I learned so much from you.

Salute to one of my mentors, Gary Charles, the founder of Advancement of Blacks in Sports (ABIS), who stamped his imprint on grassroots basketball forever when he coached Lamar Odom.

I am indebted to Athletic Director, and my former junior varsity coach, the late Mike Williams, who dared to hire me as the head varsity coach at Bishop Loughlin High School. I want to express my gratitude for my time spent working on the staff of former head coach of Bishop Loughlin, Ted Gustus. Thank You, also, to Coach Rahme Anderson, who helped me to bring in the talent needed to succeed in a reputable league like the Catholic High School Athletic Association (CHSAA).

Shout out to my best friends:

"POPE" (May Allah be pleased with you), you inspired me to reach my full potential when I was not a focused man. I appreciate your candid and real talks with me.

"House of Pain", Martin Pitts, Wayne Lassiter, and Joe Hill. We have always motivated each other because of our love for competition.

Shout out to Khalil Manigaulte and Chris Wilmore, my other brothers from my teenaged years. Thank you for keeping me grounded.

Much love to all the players, coaches, and parents who ever helped me build the brand, Brooklyn Bridge Basketball.

I must acknowledge Karon Clarke and Jamal "Tank" Dart; I consider them the "building blocks" of Bridge Nation. I put "No Limit" on the back of our team shorts because, at the time, I was a big fan of Master P. I coached both of you as hard as I could to bring out the best versions of you. Years later, it was an honor to be at the weddings of two brothers I helped make it out of Fort Greene projects in Brooklyn. It is even more of a privilege to see both of you are still best friends.

I am thankful for my New Heights Youth, Inc. family, including all the coaches and, in particular, Ted Smith, Rahme, CQ, Coach Holly, Rodney Frazier, Dominique Nute, Dan Halewicz, Adam Berkowitz, and Ashley Faison.

Thank you to...

The new head coach of Villanova University, Kyle Neptune, another player alumnus of the Brooklyn Bridge program.

Coaches/nephews/OGs I have worked with intimately in basketball: Big Reese, Ross, Kainon, Joe Robinson, 'Ice Man,' Mike Moses, DeSean, 'Cheese', 'Hollywood', Rudy King, Jay, Avalon, and Big Artie. The commitment you have made to our programs and to the lives of the young men we have coached and mentored has been priceless.

Bill Rhoden for your mentorship and for writing *Forty Million Dollar Slaves*. A lot of what I am discussing in this book was inspired by your work.

Dr. Wesley Muhammad and Wakil Muhammad, my brothers in Islam from Morehouse College. I watched both of you from afar write book after book. Your level of research and commitment to the cause has been a real inspiration for me.

The New York Knicks and the Brooklyn Nets organization for allowing me to produce, learn, and work with the best professional league in the world: the NBA.

My OG/mentor Bob Ferry with whom I traveled the country representing the Brooklyn Nets organization and who showed me nothing but respect and love by teaching jewels in the profession of scouting and evaluating talent. Rest in peace!

To the black coaches who laid the foundation for those of us who have come behind them, including John Thompson, John Cheney, Nolan Smith, John McLendon, Big "House Gaines," Lucias Mitchell, Archie Cooley, Rod Broadway, Marino Casem, Bill Ahyes, Zeke Clement, Willie Jeffries, and Eddie Robinson, to name a few.

And thank you to:

Roger Brown, from my dad's high school, Wingate

Bob Cousey and, later, Lloyd "Sweet Pea" Daniels from Andrew Jackson High School

Billy Cunningham from Erasmus Hall

Bernard King and Albert King from Ft. Greene Brooklyn, who played at Fort Hamilton High School

"Tiny" Archibald from the South Bronx and Clinton High School

Historic sites like Boys High with "Jumpin" Jackie Jackson, Connie Hawkins and Lenny Wilkins.

Years later:

Dwayne "the Pearl" Washington from Brownsville, Brooklyn

Truman High School, which featured the slick ball handling of Rod Strickland

Walter Berry from Benjamin Franklin High School

I would also like to thank

My alma mater, Bishop Loughlin, which produced Mark Jackson

Xaverian High School which produced the sharp shooting Chris Mullin

Kenny Smith, Kenny Anderson, and Brian Winters of Molloy High School

God Sham God and Ron Artest at Lasalle High School

Tina Charles, Sue Bird, and Chamique Holdsclaw of Christ the King High School

Rafer Alston out of Cardozo High School and the legendary Coach Ron Naclerio

Lloyd "World B" Free from Canarsie High School

Sidney Green out of Jefferson High School

Epihanny Prince, Shannon Bobbit, Ashanae McLaughlin, Erica Morrow and the dominating queens out of Murray Bergtraum High School

Rice High School, another powerhouse that produced Dean Meminger, Kemba Walker, Andre Barrett and Felipe Lopez as well as the legend Coach Mo Hicks

Meanwhile, Lincoln High School, gave rise to such stars as Stephon Marbury, Sebastian Tailfir, Isiah Whitehead and Lance Stephenson.

I thank all the above for leaving their stamp.

I am also grateful to my ancestors who walk with me, Popoo, Gram, Grandaddy, Grandma Dear, Pop Pop, Grandma Conchita, Mother Dear, Uncle Mike. To them I say ASE!

CONTENTS

Introduction..13

Chapter 1 - My History and Love for Sports....................................19

Chapter 2 - Introducing Players to Many Sports............................39

Chapter 3 - Keep the Fun in the Game!!...43

Chapter 4 - The Amateur Athletic Union (AAU)............................59

Chapter 5 - The Reclassification Factor..67

Chapter 6 - Choosing a High School Coach/School........................73

Chapter 7 - Specialty Sports Programs The Academy Schools........85

Chapter 8 - Coaching from the Sidelines.......................................101

Chapter 9 - The Black Student Athlete...107

Chapter 10 - Choosing a College Coach...141

Chapter 11 - HBCU Factor..155

Chapter 12 - Protect Your Player, Protect Yourself Nurture
            Your Character/ Protect Your Reputation...............169

Chapter 13 - Playing and Training...187

Chapter 14 - Self-Management, Self-Care, Video Games..............199

Post-Script The Mecca... I Thank You... 215

About the Author..219

Testimonials..221

Bibliography..223

INTRODUCTION

Throughout multiple decades that I have been in the business of basketball, I have experienced many moments that have stood out in my career. I have been blessed to have served as a Graduate Assistant at a Division I college basketball program and as head coach of a high school varsity basketball team. I have directed several Amateur Athletic Union (AAU) programs, as well as having had a nine-year role as a scout in the NBA. I am often asked questions by parents and players regarding everything from choosing a college to selecting an agent.

In this book, I have done my best to give solutions for questions that, inevitably, will come up in the many crossroads of a player's or parent's athletic journey. Specifically, I have written this book from the perspective of a black man who participated in the inner-city basketball game. I am fully aware that some of my views in this book might make some people uncomfortable; the truth can be harsh. However, I know that parents and children of all races and cultures can take something of value from this book, and I hope they do. However, first and foremost, this book was written to guide the black/brown parent and child through the minefield of AAU/Grassroots sports and beyond.

As it pertains to black and brown people, the sports industry is a unique terrain that affects us differently than it does other racial groups. Therefore, I did not ignore the political, cut-throat aspects of grassroots sports. Nor did I attempt to glorify or condemn them. I simply look at it as a part of the game that must be dealt with by having the proper knowledge, wisdom, and understanding.

This book was written for all the young black boys and girls who are conditioned systematically to see themselves from the limited view as an athlete only. They have motivated me to share some of my experiences and the wisdom I have gained from the sports industry. I want them to broaden their perception through my own lens. I hope they think much bigger than I have ever dreamed. My desire is for their dreams to include ownership and power with a black-conscious mindset. It is my ultimate wish that this book will motivate the next great black broadcaster, coach, general manager, arena contract vendor, agent, financial planner, and writer.

Since I was a little boy, I have always loved reading and writing; the creative written word represents my release. Throughout my life, my writing, including my poems, has served as my personal catharsis. Only those in my inner circle are even aware that I write poetry in which I pour my emotions—happiness, depression, anger, defiance.

Before I begin, I want to share a poem pertaining to the sports industry that is dear to me. My poem, "Run Nigga Run," is a blunt, unapologetically confrontational testament to the white supremacist way of thinking in sports as it pertains to black people, and people of color in general. This is a clap-back poem at Fox News Host Laura Ingraham who told LeBron James to "shut up and dribble."

Unfortunately, that sentiment represented the voices of many in America who think that black people are only good enough to play sports and entertain. "Run Nigga Run" is also a defiant clap-back at sportscaster Brent Musburger, who once wrote a scathing article titled, "Bizarre Protest by Smith, Carlos Tarnishes Medals," in response to Tommie Smith's and John Carlos's iconic protest moment at the 1968 Olympics. Among other things, he called them "black stormtroopers" and wrote, "Perhaps it's time 20-year-old athletes quit passing themselves off as social philosophers." Does this condescending, racist attitude sound familiar? If so, it is because Musburger and Ingraham are cut from the same cloth.

RUN NIGGA RUN
Run nigga run....
That's what they are screaming from their lungs The same ones that kill our fathers
Pay for tickets and root for sons Little Black boy and girl
You are not just here for sport and play
You are created to build
You are here to own and run things You are destined to have your say Run nigger run
We hear it louder as they get drunk They brought you here to shoot
They only recruited you here to jump Yes, you hit harder and leap further
But it is your mind when you think critically That makes them real nervous
They tell you just shut up and play Shut up and dribble
We take knees during the anthem
Cuz the times are so critical
We take stands on what we believe Then they throw us out their leagues Mahmoud Rauf
Craig Hodges
Muhammad Ali
John Carlos
Kaepernick
All just wanna get free
Run nigga run
Cuz they brought you here to entertain You bring little Johnny out his seat
You bring them amusement and fun They don't pay you to have balls They only pay you to throw a ball
As far as you can
Run fast
Run fast
Like you running from police or the Klan

Walter Scott couldn't run fast enough
Another shot down Black man
You go play in red states
Where they are proud of their red hats They screaming
MAGA, MAGA Reminiscing
When we were door mats
They hate the state
Of your black face
They stand on the soil where our fathers bled
They still screaming run nigga
Run
They only give you a slave's playbook to read Other than
that stay in your place
Run nigga run
They can use you
If you are blind, deaf, and dumb
You are a threat when you are awake
Or when you speak up like Ali
For your people
In the slums
Or when you not only say Black lives matter
But also live it and breathe it
Getting 20 points per game
But in your interviews, you talking freedom
Or choosing a Black wife
Like MJ and Juanita
Do for self like Ice Cube... Keep the money in the Black
familia?
Run Nigga Run
Yes we ready to run shit
Run shit,
We are the Kings and Queens of dynasties So please miss
us with all that dumb shit Cause when we miss a shot
Or drop a pass

We hear you yelling That we dumb as shit
But you call my same brothers your heroes
When they win you a championship
So I'm telling my people
Run nigga Run
From that hypocrisy and all that bullshit
They only love you in their uniform
But hate the uniform
You were born with RUN!!!!!

CHAPTER 1

MY HISTORY AND LOVE FOR SPORTS

Sports, and the game of basketball in particular, have always been one of the greatest loves of my life. According to my father and mother, I would bounce the ball everywhere I went: outside on the sidewalks of New York City, inside my room with the bunkbed and, every now and then, in my grandmother's living room. I loved to hear the crisp sound of the bounce. When I was finally strong and tall enough to get the ball into the ten-foot basket, I loved to hear the sound of the "swoosh." Both sounds, to my young ears, were magical, majestic, and musical.

Like many young black boys, I grew up with grandiose dreams of playing in the National Basketball Association (NBA). Growing up, my favorite players were Hall of Famers Dr. J (Julius Irving) and Isiah Thomas. I loved the Doctor because he would fly in the air with the basketball with his big fluffy afro. He was graceful and agile. He had extraordinary body control as well as supreme confidence. When my father sent me to former New York Knicks player Butch Beard's basketball camp, I wore Dr. J's white #6 Philadelphia 76ers jersey so much that it began to stand up by itself. By the end of the week, that jersey had developed a fragrance that would never make it on the Macy's cologne shelves. Dr. J was my first superhero!

As I got more serious with the game, I fell in love with Isiah Thomas. Isiah exemplified toughness. He came from Chicago, like my mother and her side of the family. Chicago is a city known for people who have strength and grit. Isiah exemplified those qualities, but he was also a wizard with the basketball. He stood at only six-foot-one, yet he was a "giant" on the court. A sophomore in 1981, he led the University of Indiana to an NCAA Championship. In the NBA, he was the ringleader of the "Bad Boys," the nickname given to the Detroit Pistons for their rough and physical style of play. The Bad Boys won two Championships: in 1988-1989 and 1989-1990. Thomas was enshrined into the Hall of Fame in the year 2000.

Dr. J and Isiah represented some of the best that black people had to offer in the world of sports. Early in my psyche, I knew that representation mattered. Those brothers and I had the same melanin and had a walk and talk that was relatable. My mother approved of these brothers because they were articulate during interviews and served as positive role models for her little boy. Though I wanted to be an NBA player, I'm pretty sure the idea of becoming a coach crossed my young mind at times. I don't remember too many coaches in the NBA who looked like me when I was growing up, and I certainly was not aware of the other professions that existed in the sports industry. In my youth, only the players mattered in my eyes.

I came of age in the 1980s and early '90s. I was raised during the Ronald Reagan era, when crack began to make its evil way into the inner cities of the United States. Hell's Kitchen is on the west side of Manhattan and includes 42nd Street and the Times Square area. That area was flooded with pimps and prostitutes at the time and was a dangerous place to be. Of course, this was way before *The Lion King*, 5 Guys, or the ice cream store Cold Stone Creamery came to Broadway.

In this era, Dave Winfield played for the Yankees, Muhammad Ali was fighting his last few fights, and welterweight legend Sugar Ray Leonard was in his prime. Hulk Hogan was the WWE Champ and Ed Koch was the mayor of NYC. Sugar Hill, Kurtis Blow, Afrika Bambaattaa, and the Zulu Nation were bumping out of the speakers of boomboxes on the shoulders of brothers all over. As hip hop became the standard music of my culture, nothing brought home my love for a sport like the hit single "Basketball" by Kurtis Blow:

Basketball is my favorite sport
I like the way they dribble up and down the court Just like
I'm the king on the microphone
So is Dr. J and Moses Malone
I like slam dunks, take me to the hoop
My favorite play is the alley-oop
I like the pick-and-roll, I like the give-and-go Cause it's
basketball...
—Kurtis Blow

I remember so much from that era. However, nothing stands out more than when my mother took her little guy on an Amtrak train to see Dr. J and the 76ers play against Sidney Moncrief and the Milwaukee Bucks in the NBA playoffs. YES! I was finally going to see the Doctor play. I could not sleep the night before the game. My imagination went wild; I really believed I was going to meet him. I thought he might even teach me how to play and jump like him. Maybe, just maybe, he would even marry my mother! Seriously, this is what I was thinking.

Needless to say, none of these things ever came to fruition. However, when I got to see him play, it was every bit of the treat that I imagined. He was so smooth. He played in the air. He walked with a swag and a confidence that I would later find out as a coach would be hard to teach. After seeing him compete, I would pattern my style of play completely after his. Later, I came to realize that there were many things as players that we would never have in common. He was a forward and I was a guard. He was six-feet-six inches and I would only grow to be five-feet-six. Dr. J mastered things well above the rim. I would have to carve my niche as a player well below the basket.

I spent my teens primarily in Brooklyn, New York, but I also spent the beginning stages of my childhood in Hell's Kitchen, on 43rd Street and 9th Avenue in Manhattan Plaza. Manhattan Plaza was a residential building designated for performing artists. Stars such as Alicia Keys, Terrence Howard and Donald Faison grew up in this complex. Even the great actor Samuel Jackson worked in the complex as a security guard for a while.

My mother enrolled me in a sports program called the Champions, comprised mostly of working and middle-class youth. Most of the children in the program were white and very few were black. We played against other groups consisting of the same socioeconomic and racial makeup. However, the Champions had the highest demographic of black and brown children in the entire league. One of my white peers was Mike Rapaport, the accomplished actor.

I excelled as an athlete in the Champions program. At every awards banquet, I knew I would receive at least one or two awards in the sports I played which included football, basketball and baseball. The coaches of all the teams I played for meant a lot to me during this period. Many served as role models as my father's participation in my life was spotty at times. My father was a newly-elected State Assemblyman in the 57 District in Brooklyn. He struggled at times with the demands of his profession and his duty as a father. Eventually, he grew to be a giant in both roles.

In addition to my mother, and paternal grandfather, my coaches represented real stability. I knew that every Saturday I had a game or practice and I relied on my coaches for leadership. I loved the candid conversations I had with them, especially when I was given advice on topics that ranged from girls to life in general. Later on in this book, I will address the importance of selecting the right coach.

Usually, while playing for the Champions, we beat the other teams in the league; however, when we competed against the prominent AAU programs, such as the legendary Gauchos or Riverside Church programs, we got pummeled—often. I remember one particular day when we played against the Gauchos. We did not do well, according to the scoreboard, but I played well individually. I was not especially tall, yet I was fast, quick, and passionate. Once I got past the first defender off the dribble, I could score usually by making lay-ups and I was good at making the right pass.

After one game in particular, my father was approached by opposing Gauchos coaches. They invited me to come down and play for them. I guess this was my first introduction into grassroots basketball recruiting. After contemplating the offer, my father denied the request. Later, he told me he made the decision because he had heard about some shady stuff going on with the "The 'Choz," and he did not want me to get involved. Ironically, years later, as an AAU director and coach, they would become one of my greatest rivals.

As I look back on my basketball life, my father's apprehension about accepting the Gauchos' invitation was both good and bad. The positive takeaway was that my father was shielding me from some of the negative aspects of the grassroots basketball world. Grassroots often has the feel and pace of the streets. It is one big rat race, and everyone is trying to finish in first place. There are no real rules. Similar to the drug game, a basketball program is only as good as the product you put out. The product in this space are the players. Though my father's presence in my life was inconsistent in my childhood, this was one of my cherished moments where he was displaying a level of protection.

The negative effect of his decision was that it kept me from competing consistently against the best players in the city. This would have taken me out of my comfort zone, a necessity in order to excel in anything in life. He preferred to keep me with the Champions program and continue on the steady and slow approach to amateur basketball, as opposed to the sprint approach that engulfs most of the youth basketball world today. For better or worse, the Champions would remain my athletic home until I got to junior high school.

MOVING TO BROOKLYN

When I was about 12 years old, I moved, abruptly, to Brooklyn. Out of pure survival, we had to move for the sake of our peace of mind. We went to stay with my paternal grandparents, "Popoo" and "Dear," in Crown Heights, Brooklyn. As I reflect on this move now, my mother probably had to exhibit a tremendous amount of humility to make this move. I will be forever thankful to my grandparents for welcoming us into their home, even though my parents were divorced. This move inevitably broke up the consistency of practice and playing that I had lived for each and every Saturday with the Champions program. Though I still loved the game, I had no sports structure anymore.

Now, I was literally a lost boy in the wilderness of Brooklyn, USA. This was the '80s, way before the overt push to gentrify Kings County. This was the beginning of the crack era, which ravaged the black community, similar to how heroin and opioid addiction is ravaging white suburbia today. In Brooklyn in the '80s, it was nor- mal to walk down the street and see used blue, red, and black crack vials on the pavement. In a *Daily News* article written by Gene Mustain titled "When the crack scourge swept New York City," he explains,

"In 1988 by several measures, the city was brought to its knees. It was the worst year ever for murder; nearly 40% of the 1,896 homicides were drug-related, meaning mainly crack-related. It was the worst year ever for total violent crimes...murder, plus robbery and assault. The violent-crime total, 152,600, meant that New York had as many victims as Syracuse had people."

Crack took a more personal toll on my family as it wiped away the lives of my cousin, Janice, and her husband, Willie, leaving my great-aunt to raise her children.

In my impressionable mind, Dr. J's superstar status was slowly being replaced by neighborhood names such as "Supreme Magnetic,"

"Killer Ben," "Fat Cat," "Alpo," "Phil," and "Pat." These guys were not shooting basketballs, but their swag matched The Doctor's. They wore "truck" big rope jewelry; three- and four-finger gold rings; slick waved hair with the half-moon part; and, they drove around in flashy BMWs and Mercedes Benzes. They were big-time drug dealers that were "breaking news" in the hood way before CNN was ever recognized for doing the same. I would hear stories often of a club uptown called the Rooftop in Harlem, or the impromptu car shows that took place in front of Willie Burgers.

In this era, like many before and after, the hustlers attracted the finest girls who wore big gold door-knocker earrings, crispy bangs that hung in front of their foreheads, sleek gelled-down baby hairs with Dippity Do gel, shiny gold frames in the teeth, fresh clean sneakers, and Cazal glasses. The lure of the streets is almost undefeated in the inner cities of America. The smoke-and-mirror illusion of the hood produces a magnetic pull that can take even some of the best-raised young boys or girls and turn them inside out.

My mother reminds me often of the time she was talking to me in the car, but I wasn't paying attention because I was distracted. She said that my head and eyes were fixated on the dope boys on the corner. My mother knew at that moment how impressionable the streets could be. She knew I was vulnerable to that gravitational pull. These brothers I was staring at commanded respect and had young soldiers they employed. They had an enormous presence like they were the CEOs of the block. I was attracted to that look of power.

Meanwhile, as the hip-hop scene continued to progress, Eric B and Rakim, Kool G Rap, KRS - One, NWA, and Public Enemy began to boom from car speakers. I would hear terms like "Peace God" while hearing about mathematics from a whole different perspective from brothers of the Five Percent Nation. Violence in the communities became more common. In the basketball world, Bernard King, who was raised in the Ft. Greene section of Brooklyn, was getting buckets for the Knicks. This was New York City, filled with grit and with an edge. I am very blessed to have survived Brooklyn in the '80s as a youth. I know of a lot of brothers and sisters who did not.

The lack of sports in my life during this time often caused me to slip back and forth between having a civilized mentality and that of a savage. My mother, an activist, performing artist, and college professor divorced my father when I was in grade school. She worked days, evenings and weekends teaching classes to make ends meet. Balancing work, home life, her art and me was no easy feat. I know that now. And her absence gave the latchkey, headstrong boy that I was enough time to find loopholes in her parenting system.

Once I finished my homework, I was off to hang out with a new group of friends in the Crown Heights section of Brooklyn. These brothers introduced me to a new culture that I was not aware of prior to meeting them. They spoke with a deeper slang; their thought patterns were faster. They were much slicker than some of my peers that I grew up with in Hell's Kitchen. They had seen things at thirteen and fourteen years old that young boys should never have to witness. In the rough streets of Brooklyn, a thirteen-year-old boy or girl can easily have the mindset of someone seventeen or eighteen years old. I, on the other hand, had the mentality of a true thirteen- or fourteen-year-old, and my new friends knew it right away. I was "green," and I had to learn the ways and norms of this new culture.

This way of life meant slap boxing, drinking Cisco, talking shit, boosting, shoplifting, fighting, and jonsing with more ruthless "mama jokes." It also meant learning to play cee-lo, the dice game that originated in Brooklyn. I also had to learn new body language, which allowed me to perceive danger or non-danger at a moment's notice. To my surprise, some of the principles my mama raised me with translated to the streets. She taught me early in life to walk with my chest out, chin up, and look a man in his eyes when he talks. I was also taught to give firm handshakes and always speak with confidence.

I needed every one of those lessons when going to a playground full of brothers. The park environment is where I learned quickly to grow up. There were people shooting dice, selling drugs, playing music, and so forth. The park was a who's who of all the characters in the hood. It was full of ball players, drug dealers, stick-up boys, regular brothers, and those who straddled the fence like me. In PS11 park, one of the parks I grew up in, Christopher Wallace would grow up to become one of the greatest hip hop MCs that ever walked the planet. He would later be known all over the world as the Notorious Biggie Smalls.

With all this testosterone in the park, one question that is really simple, yet pertinent, to every basketball player in the hood is "Who has next?" My scrawny, short body needed to have the heart to ask the question with some "umph" in my tone. If done with any trepidation or fear, it could be dismissed easily, or I could even face some type of disrespect for not speaking with some base in my voice. Therefore, I had to speak with confidence, and with my chest out, when I was on the sidelines with all the brothers looking on.

I needed that same heart and self-assured conviction when 'my boys' and I would go from one community to another to play against different tribes, as we often did. I remember vividly how we would plan a best-out-of-five-games series like it was the NBA playoffs. We played against a lot of brothers who would one day get caught up deep in the streets. In particular, one of my opponents would miss over fifteen years of his childhood after he was charged for murder. In retrospect, the prospects of our futures never really crossed our young minds at the time. All we wanted to do was compete against each other and play the game of basketball.

BISHOP LOUGHLIN HIGH SCHOOL

I moved into my father's house during my freshman year at Bishop Loughlin High School. I appreciated growing up with my mother and the work she put into my development; however, I started tuning out her voice. I longed for a meaningful relationship with my father and, for the rest of my life, it proved to be priceless.

I am a firm believer that a woman cannot show a boy how to be a man, just as a man cannot demonstrate to a young girl how to be a woman. This is different from teaching the skills of adulthood. Like many young boys, I grew up without a father in the home. I was blessed to form the relationship that I still have with my dad. His very presence at my games made me feel loved. His support meant that I mattered in his eyes, and it began to heal the scars that were inflicted earlier in my childhood. Needless to say, my self-esteem was raised when he re-established himself in my life.

In the spring of my freshman season, my dad did a great job of researching basketball camps. We both knew that I had to enhance my skills. Most notably, I needed to improve dribbling with my left hand. I also needed to develop a consistent jump shot. Staring at me in the face was the junior varsity team that I wanted to join. Junior was coached by the pitch black-skinned, almost six-feet-two, intimidating at times, Mike Williams. He had a background of coaching at the collegiate level and a reputation for imposing strict discipline on his players. I knew I had to be ready for this challenge.

My father began to set up a routine of working on my game a couple days a week. We would go to the local college (Pratt Institute) after school, and I would work on my weaknesses. My father was studious, looking up drills that would enhance my game. He put me through left-handed passing drills; he made me shoot off the dribble, make free-throws and the like. I did not realize it at the time but, besides the priceless moments he spent with me, my father smelled a decrease in tuition or even a full college scholarship in the air. The weekly workouts prepared me for the basketball camps he would send me to during the summer.

The summer of my rising sophomore year, I went to Hall of Fame high school coach Morgan Wooten's camp in Maryland. I attended Georgia Tech's basketball camp, led by head coach Bobby Cremins who, at the time, was recruiting NYC point guard legend Kenny Anderson. Kenny, though older, played in the same league as I did at Molly High School in Queens. I also participated in The University of Louisville basketball camp. I specifically worked on my shooting mechanics at Dick Baumgartner's shooting camp in Richmond, Indiana. The highlight of all the camps was the Syracuse Basketball Camp where I hung with all the brothers from Brooklyn. We gravitated towards each other in the cafeteria, and we showed support for each other at our respective games.

The youngest one of us received more attention from the Syracuse coaching staff than anyone in the group. He was about eleven years old when I was fifteen. He was diminutive in stature and was very jovial and playful like the rest of the group. On one day in particular, this young boy asked us if we wanted to go hang with him off campus. Of course, we obliged, and we visited the house of one of the Syracuse assistant coaches. We had a good time eating and cracking jokes. When I left the house, I remember being "blessed" with Syracuse gear to take back to the dorm. While I received a few things, it was nowhere near the amount of stuff that this young boy received. I didn't realize it then, but this was my first introduction to the privilege that comes with having a special talent. The formula is very simple: if you have a special set of skills—in this country and globally—you will get special treatment.

The young brother I am referring to was on another level when it came to the game of basketball. He was too advanced for his own age group in the camp, so he played in my division and more than held his own. He dominated with minimum effort. He did things on the court that I have only seen the pros do on television. He played like an NBA player, and later he became one. His name was Stephon Marbury.

Eventually, he became a high school All-American at the New York City powerhouse Lincoln High School in Coney Island, Brooklyn.

Many years later, I would win a PSAL championship as an assistant coach for the same program. Stephon would go on to play in the NBA for fourteen years before playing in China, where he reached iconic status because of his performances on the court and his contributions to the country off the court.

I played two more seasons at Bishop Loughlin before moving to Thomaston, Georgia, where I spent my senior year at Upson High School. Thomaston is located a little over an hour's drive south of Atlanta; a rural town, its economy was based in the Thomaston Textile Mills. I used to spend parts of my summers there as a child with my family, including my great-grandfather, Pop Pop, who once pitched in the Negro Baseball Leagues. He was married to my feisty but lovable great-grandmother, Gram.

Prior to moving back to Georgia, Gram was a domestic worker for a wealthy white family in the Lincoln Park section of Chicago. Among her duties was the cleaning of the floors of their homes on her knees, yet my mother talks with pride when she remembers Gram teaching her high-level domestic skills and imploring her to live life with a sense of dignity, self-respect, and pride. This beautiful queen was my heart and the undisputed GOAT (Greatest Of All Time) cook of the family.

I have vivid memories from my senior year in that town. I saw Confederate flags on the backs of trucks that drove down red dirt roads. The only other school besides mine in the area was named after the Confederate General Robert E. Lee. The southern drawl and submissive body language of many of my classmates was very foreign to me. The condescending manner with which white people communicated with black people in that town left a nasty taste in my mouth.

On the other hand, the warmth and love I felt in that home was unmatched. I would come home to the smell of beef ribs, home-made mashed potatoes, collard greens, barbeque, and fried chicken. Every meal smelled good; however, there was one exception: the death odor that filled my nostrils from the cooking of pig guts, better known as chitterlings.

My basketball season in Georgia did not go as well as I wanted. I was a starter on the team and had decent numbers, but I underesti-mated the adjustments I would have to make on a new team. I also had set unrealistic goals for myself. These expectations put more pressure on me than I needed in my senior year. I did a lot of overthinking and became my worst opponent at times. Years later, I would sense that same anxiety in some of the unsigned seniors I coached.

Even worse, I did not handle my recruitment process well. I was being recruited by Division II coaches in the area, but I lacked interest in these programs. I was not feeling the coaches who were pursuing me. I also dropped the ball with my correspondence with these coaches and even avoided some of their phone calls. I handled the process unprofessionally. It didn't help that I was away from my father; he would have certainly helped ease my confusion. Without leadership I was totally unprepared and overwhelmed.

While I was in Thomaston, I would travel to Atlanta often on the weekends when I did not have practice or games. I would sleep on the floor of my best friend Khalil's freshman dorm. I hung out with him and a couple of his boys. I was slowly getting acclimated to Atlanta University's culture, and I loved it. I did not receive interest from Morehouse College coaches, but it didn't matter. When I received my Morehouse acceptance letter in the mail, I knew that was where I was going. As for my senior season in high school, my team won a lot of games, but we fell short of the championship we were expect-ing to win. In hindsight, I probably should not have transferred my senior year.

COLLEGE...AND BEYOND

I did not play basketball in college due to my extracurricular activities, which included heavy drinking, excessive weed smoking, and other things that I will save for another book. Just know that it was a REAL miracle that I even graduated.

Upon leaving Morehouse College with a degree in Health and Physical Education, I enrolled at Long Island University where I earned a Masters in English while working for Head Men's Basketball Coach Ray Haskins. It was my first opportunity to work in college athletics. He grew up with my father in Bedford Stuyvesant (Bed-Stuy) neighborhood of Brooklyn. Coach Haskins was the right fit for me as a mentor, since I was a little rough around the edges and he is what I would consider a "man's man" who walked with a sense of conviction and pride.

He wore glasses, was stout and stood at five-feet-ten. He was unapologetically black. In his small office, pictures of Dr. Martin Luther King and Malcolm X hung on his wall. He also had an office full of candy jars, from which I feasted regularly. Those sugar wafers used to call my name. As an aspiring young coach, it was a blessing to be around Coach Haskins. I learned the bulk of my defensive and offensive schemes from this man. In his practices, he stressed the intricacies of the game, such as taking charges, flicking, and making free-throws under pressure.

He was a successful coach prior to joining LIU, having won multiple PSAL championships at Alexander Hamilton High School in Brooklyn. He used the same method to build a successful college program. In addition to the system, we had very good players, including the nation's leading scorer at the time, Charles Jones, who transferred from Rutgers University. Coach Haskins was a psychological master. He used to sit Charles when he did not shoot the ball. That philosophy obviously worked as Charles led the nation in scoring with 29.9 points per game that year.

Overall, my first year as a graduate assistant was a success. We played in the Northeast Conference, which is a league where only the conference tournament champion is usually represented in the NCAA Tournament. Our record was 21-8 in the 1997 season. Eventually, we won our conference tournament, beating Monmouth University 72-67. I will never forget the crowd running onto the court and our team cutting the nets after that momentous game.

Unfortunately, we lost in the first round of the NCAA Tournament to Villanova, which was led by freshman Tim Thomas. Later, Thomas became an NBA player. I remember we made our runs in the game with a wave of three pointers coming from some of our shooters on the team. We did not have enough talent to match the other players that were supporting Tim Thomas. The next year, we lost in the conference tournament to Farleigh Dickinson. I was devastated; I thought it was a foregone conclusion that we would win again. It felt like a big balloon had been popped in the game and all the air that let out also drained the oxygen out of our team. Despite that setback, we did get invited to the National Invitational Tournament (NIT), where we played and lost to Dayton University, which had an amazing home court advantage.

GRASSROOTS BASKETBALL

During the summer of 1998, I began to make my way into the world of grassroots basketball. With the help of my father, who at the time was a State Assemblyman and activist in Central Brooklyn, I founded and coached a program called Brooklyn Bridge Basketball. My friend, Khalil, handled the day-to-day operations of our program while I focused on coaching. Most of the players we recruited came from the Ft. Greene section of Brooklyn and Bed-Stuy where the environments are tough. Numerous obstacles put them at an inherent disadvantage, including subpar schools, poverty, and rampant drug use, as well as gun violence. Many of the children are talented yet need to be guided and assisted with their purpose and focus.

My teams often played in local tournaments usually riddled with ringers in every division. We were a twelve-years-old and under team. It was not uncommon for us to compete against players who were fourteen and sometimes even fifteen years old. During that time, and even now in Brooklyn tournaments, thirteen was the new twelve. I competed often against coaches who did not care to honor the age requirements of particular tournaments. Many coaches only cared about putting their team in a position to get a trophy, even if it was at the expense of their integrity. This was, and often still is, the wilderness of Brooklyn basketball, where everything and almost anything goes.

As I took on the role of coach in my early twenties, I also assumed an even bigger role that eventually would fulfill my soul in a much deeper way. This was as a mentor and big brother. Many of the boys I coached had no dad in the home. Therefore, I became a young father figure— immediately. I must admit, this heightened my sense of responsibility and I needed to set a dignified example for young men. However, I was also fighting my own personal demons. I was an active alcoholic, a big fan of Hennessy and Alizé. This was the Cognac combination that Tupac would make famous by calling it "Thug Passion." I also smoked weed during this time. Often, I would be a little buzzed before some games, with a hint of liquor on my breath. Many times, I would wake up for a Sunday game with a hangover.

My stubbornness and resilience actually worked against me, as I did my best to solve this drinking Rubik's cube by myself. No matter how hard I tried to drink a little or only consume on some days and not others, I failed. When I tried to completely stop I failed miserably, not making it past two weeks at the most. It was not until I saw my younger cousin come home from rehab looking clean and healthy that I saw an example of something I wanted for myself. Eventually, I decided to take the same route as my cousin and checked myself into rehab to get the help I needed. It has since proved to be one of the best decisions I have ever made. It saved me from drowning, literally, in alcohol.

When I gave up drinking, my passion and focus picked up. Coaching basketball and helping young black men would be how I fulfilled my purpose. Coaching and winning games while sober allowed me to find a new, natural euphoria. My intensity and passion for coaching increased; I loved to win but being sober meant that I was winning in life. I believe I was able to demand more respect from my players and I was held in higher regard by their parents. Yes, I have always been a person who hated to lose, with a passion. Embracing sobriety meant that I was no longer a failure.

My passion was on full display when I coached in the pre-teen championship at 305 Park in Bed-Stuy. My team had a lead over Brooklyn USA, our rival at the time. We squandered the lead and ended up losing the game. As I talked to the team, with a heavy scent of weed blowing in the air from the onlookers in the park, I broke down in tears. I was hurting big time from the loss. While the defeat was disappointing, the pain was sharper than usual because I no longer had alcohol to mask my raw feelings. At that moment in time, I felt like I had lost the NCAA National Championship.

The next year, I did a good job of recruiting more thirteen-year-old boys to go along with the core players I already had. Also, with the help of Khalil and my father, I began to create a family-like environment for the boys. We spent a lot of time together off the court, which enhanced our chemistry as a team. We ate together like a family, we took them to college basketball games, and had candid conversations with our boys about life. This would be the formula for success that I have used throughout my coaching career.

As I went on to become a high school coach and AAU director/coach, I noticed a severe lack of participation from fathers for a variety of reasons. As a coach, I believe it is my duty to fill that void mentally, emotionally and, at times, financially— the same way my coaches had done for me.

As the years continued, I coached with a fire that, I admit, was at times nasty. I was not always cordial with opposing coaches, nor towards some of my own players and opposing fans, and I had a temper that often I could not control. On one occasion, my temper almost cost me my head coaching job at Bishop Loughlin. Prior to getting hired as the head varsity coach, I coached the freshman team. My former JV coach, Mike Williams, was the athletic director. When the previous varsity head coach stepped down, it was widely thought that the long-standing JV coach would get the job. The coach had won a lot of games with the powerhouse Riverside Church.

As time went by and the school started interviewing candidates from outside of its campus, I felt I deserved to be considered for the position. Needless to say, this caused unspoken tension between the JV coach and me though, to be transparent, I told him what I would be doing.

When it was announced that I got the job, I was ecstatic. It was time to show and prove what I could do under the bright lights of the CHSAA. My hiring caused inevitable strain between me and some of the parents who were pushing for the coach to get the position. There were rumors that some parents were going to have their sons transfer to other schools. In retrospect, I should not have taken this personally because players often transfer when a new coach takes over a program.

One parent was the father of a junior who went on to play Division I college basketball at Fairfield University. One day, my meeting with the team went overtime as we discussed our recent losing streak. His father was waiting on him in the hallway and apparently was running out of patience with our meeting.

Soon, he started banging on the classroom door like the police do before serving a warrant. As he grew more irritated about the length of our meeting, so did I with his banging. Finally, my anger got the best of me. I burst out of the door and screamed, "WHAT THE FUCK IS WRONG WITH YOU!?" As my coaches tried to intervene by holding me back physically, I did my best to get out of their grasp and I attacked him. I knew he never wanted to see me become his son's head coach and, finally, our underlying resentment towards one another came to a head. I wanted to beat his ass and I lost control of my emotions.

The next day, I had to meet with the principal to explain my side of the story and apologize for my actions. I was embarrassed for myself and for the people who had supported my getting the job. I was aware immediately that I had to clean up my side of the street. Eventually, I apologized to the parent for my role in the incident and, for the rest of his son's career at the school, he and I treated each other with respect. As I look back, I can honestly say that I am glad to have learned hard lessons regarding coaching etiquette prior to the advent of video cameras and social media. Otherwise, I would never have made it as far as I have. My wings would have been clipped before I had made it off the launching pad.

CHAPTER 2

INTRODUCING PLAYERS TO MANY SPORTS

As I mentioned earlier, I played for The Champions sports club, where I competed seasonally in football, basketball, and baseball. I must say I was pretty good in all three sports. I used my agility and speed to excel in baseball which is a precise sport. I played the outfield and usually batted first in the line-up because I was good at getting on base. I was the setup man, and I loved stealing bases. One of my idols was Ricky Henderson of the Oakland A's, who currently holds the Major League Baseball record for stolen bases and is in the Hall of Fame. Ricky could dominate a game as soon as he got on base. His very presence could throw a nervous pitcher completely off their game. I wanted to have this effect as a baserunner.

Football enhanced my mental and physical toughness. I remember playing in freezing cold temperatures. My mother would often be near, watching the game while sipping hot chocolate in our old Volvo that had faulty brakes and no heat. My mother's support was unwavering. I played offense and defense in football. On defense, I played free safety. On a blitz, my favorite thing to do was to hit the quarterback like the legendary Lawrence Taylor of the New York Giants would do when he played. "LT," as he was referred to, was another athlete that I grew up watching and admiring.

I was a very active boy. I even took tennis classes and won a match. At the time, John McEnroe and Bjorn Borg were at the top of the male tennis scene. I loved watching the flare of Yannick Noah, the black man from France who won the French Open in 1983. How ironic it is that, years later, I coached his son, Joakim, with the nationally acclaimed NY Panthers' grassroots basketball program.

One year, we participated in the Bob Gibbons AAU basketball tournament in North Carolina. After the tournament, I drove back to New York City in my small Mitsubishi Galant with Joakim. Can you imagine a seven-footer riding shotgun and turning my front seat into a back seat? Well, yeah, that's how we rolled for about eight hours on the highway (one of the duties that came with being an assistant coach). Years later, Joakim would make our Panther organization proud by winning two national championships at the University of Florida. Later, he became a two-time NBA All-Star, as well as the NBA Defensive Player of the Year in 2014.

Playing multiple sports gave me an appreciation for athletes of all genres. There is so much sacrifice and discipline that goes into each craft. I did not realize it at the time, but my participation was helping me train different muscles. According to Michelle Smith's article for *ESPN.com* in 2016, "Studies show that playing multiple sports leads to better muscle, motor, and skill development. It promotes general athleticism, balance, speed, and agility." There are many sports to participate in, and I think it is a very narrow approach to limit a child's experience to one sport.

Jackie Robinson is known for the legacy he left in Major League Baseball. However, many people do not know that his best sport was basketball. He was known to be so quick and fast that he was nicknamed "Black Lightning." He also played football, ran track and field, and lettered in four sports at UCLA. Although he reached the Hall of Fame for baseball, many people say that actually it was his worst sport.

Of course, there are other world class athletes who played multiple sports in their youth. Michael Jordan is the greatest basketball player to ever walk the earth, in my opinion, but he also played baseball and ran track in his youth. Gordon Hayward, the all-star forward for the Charlotte Hornets, grew up playing tennis. Elena Delle Donne competed in volleyball at the University of Delaware before returning to the basketball team and later becoming a two-time WNBA MVP. Derek Jeter, arguably one of the best shortstops

CHAPTER 3

KEEP THE FUN IN THE GAME!!

When you are introducing your child to any sport like soccer or basketball, ask yourself: Does your child have the attention span to play those sports for an entire game? Does he share with others? Is she physically coordinated? What do you want him or her to get out of the sport, besides playing?

There are so many intangibles and values to be gained from any sport you choose. I strongly urge parents to research the game *before* you get into it. As a parent, you know your child best. It is your job to set the athletic table so they can eat from a holistic perspective. Remember, this is your child's first introduction to athletics. All sports are just games; initially, all games are made to bring a natural high to the brain. They are meant to bring joy as well as to challenge.

When I first started playing sports, I formed a personal relationship with each ball I played with as if it was a new teddy bear. I used to walk everywhere with a football. I tucked it under my arms, as my coach encouraged me to do to help prevent me from fumbling. I used to bounce the basketball when I walked to the store for my mother so that I could work on my handle. I was displaying an early commitment to the sport, while also expressing my affection. This is the same passion and love I see in many of the seven- and eight-year-old children who come into "the Foundation," a development program I run for New Heights. They often enter our gym with big eyes, as they bounce the ball, big "Kool-Aid" smiles on their faces. They show a pure and innocent relationship to the game; their eyes demonstrate a strong desire to stay on the journey.

In the '90s, impressionable and thirsty young ball players wanted desperately to "be like Mike," as expressed in the Gatorade marketing campaign featuring Michael Jordan. The new wave of children now has ambitions to be like Steph Curry, or A'ja Wilson of the Las Vegas Aces in the WNBA. As the young player grows in the game, the demands of the sport will grow. The competitive portion of the game can be consuming. These days, children are getting ranked at an early age and they and their parents hope that they can become the next Kyrie Irving or Trae Young.

As a parent, you will begin spending entire weekends watching your son or daughter play, which can be a very stressful experience for your child, their teammates, the coach and you. Your child is trying to shoot a pressure free throw or make the right play with time dwindling on the game clock. On top of this, the training, uniforms, travel, lodging and food are costly. Parents, I implore you, do not to forget the reason your child started playing in the first place: for the love and the fun of the game.

According to John O'Sullivan, author of *Changing the Game*, more than 70 percent of young athletes drop out of organized sports before reaching high school, largely because it is no longer fun. Kids are being pushed to "be on travel teams by age 7, have a private coach by 8, and be committed to a single sport by 10." The myth that sports will provide scholarships or entry into elite universities for everyone who participates has helped create this culture. I have seen parents single-handedly dim the pure light in their child's eyes with the pressure they placed on him or her. I have witnessed fathers curse their sons out for poor performance in front of their teammates. The embarrassed look on that child's face would be the beginning of many mental wounds that he would walk around with forever.

I have had parents take their children off my team in the middle of a tournament, due to a lack of playing time. Hence, they are teaching their sons to quit and not stick things out until the end. In my opinion, these parent-centered decisions lead to emotional scars, shattering the mental toughness and fight their children will need in a larger game, the game of life.

I strongly urge parents and coaches not to let anything get in the way of your child's foundational love for sports. Do not forget about all the priceless intangibles that your child can gain from healthy competition. They can gain a strong sense of discipline, long-lasting friendships, and increased self-esteem. The game can be tough on their psyche—no different than life—and the skills developed through this process can be priceless.

Do not let your ego get in the way of your child's development. Comparing your son's or daughter's development to that of their peers is always detrimental. Never forget that children do not all develop at the same pace. Too much ego can get in the way of progress. The meditation guru Deepak Chopra gave the word ego the acronym "EDGING GOD OUT." I don't want to get too deep but, in this instance, God represents the source of one's pure love for the game. The longer your child grows in the sport, the more you will need to keep nurturing the original seed that was planted when your child fell in love. Do not ever forget that first basket that your child made in a game and the joy it brought him. More importantly, don't let him forget it. That first basket was just one more way of nurturing the original seed of love!

I have also seen envy and jealousy creep slowly into a parent's mindset and inevitably find its way to their offspring. In team competition, parents sometimes forget that their child has to coexist with the entire team in a fluid and balanced manner. Everyone's journey is different. Do not compare your child with others. It is better to measure his/her own progress with themselves. The elite teams and the best players understand that no matter how confident and/or good they become, they must also maintain a sense of humility.

Parents must learn to differentiate their dreams as a parent from the wants and desires of the child. Parents must take the time to get on the same page as their child. Sit down with him/her and ask what they want out of the sport. Do not ignore their feelings! Remember this is their show. The parent is there to guide and protect.

FINDING THE RIGHT EARLY DEVELOPMENTAL COACH

Finding the right developmental coach is probably one of the most important things a parent can do. Your child's coach will have a tremendous influence on his mental, physical, and emotional well-being. He/she will depend on the coach you have selected to teach them the fundamentals of the game. Good coaches are good teachers first. They should have a mastery of their craft and know how to transfer what they know to their students/players through proper communication.

I learned a lot in a coaching class when I attended Morehouse. Almost 25 years later, I now teach a class on coaching at Long Island University (LIU). A young man in the legendary Brooklyn coach Ray Haskins' practice sessions, I would write down every drill and play I could learn. I was eager to apply what I learned so I could instruct, teach, and coach young boys from my community.

Later, I became an assistant coach at Benjamin Banneker HS, Lincoln HS, and Bishop Loughlin HS before ultimately taking the varsity head coaching job at Bishop Loughlin. Through my entire coaching journey and in life in general, I have been open to learning from anyone. I have sat in on many college and NBA practices, studied endless hours of video, and attended many coaching clinics.

When I was a part-time scout for the New Jersey Nets prior to becoming full-time with the Brooklyn Nets, I learned so much from head coach Lawrence Frank regarding his defensive philosophy. He taught the importance of "shrinking" the floor from a defensive stand- point. I have read John Thompson's book I *Came as a Shadow*, *Forty Minutes of Hell*, about the life of the legendary Nolan Richardson, Pat Riley's book *The Winner Within*, and *Finding a Way* to *Win* by Bill Parcells. I adopted some of their leadership styles, coaching techniques, and strategies to hone my craft. I incorporated an efficient secondary offense from the late, great Morgan Wooten. I also implemented elements of the Temple "match-up zone" from the legendary head coach, John Chaney. I certainly consider myself a student of the game, and I have learned plenty from personal experience as well.

When looking for the right coach, make sure they can articulate to you their basketball experiences. Here are some questions you can ask them:

- Where did you learn your concepts in coaching?

- Have you played before? At what levels?

- How do you develop your players?

- Are practices open to parents? (If so, attend a practice and observe their patience, temperament, and structure)

- What made you get into coaching?

Parents of an eight- to ten-year-old player will want their child's first experience with the sport to be as comfortable as possible, the less intimidating, the better. Many grassroots programs do not have the resources to pay good quality youth coaches and many experienced people who have the desire to coach, do not have the time. Often, this leads to parents volunteering in some capacity. If they love sports like most of us do, they will get that "itch" which could lead them to taking stats for the team, taping games/practices or, ultimately, coaching.

In my opinion, on MOST occasions, fathers should not coach their own sons. Let me preface my opinion by stating this does not apply to ALL FATHERS; as the saying goes, "if it don't apply, let it fly." However, I must be honest: from what I have witnessed on many occasions, the dynamic of fathers coaching their sons has been crippling to the young man's development. I know many fathers who don't know how to take off the father hat to be an objective coach with their team. The lines are often blurred. Either they are way too hard on their sons when they play for them or way too soft. Rarely have I witnessed a healthy balance. That is why many programs prohibit parents from coaching their own children and I totally agree. I would not recommend any parent putting their child in this team dynamic. Of course, in some circumstances the situation is unavoidable but, if possible, find another way.

As the current director of community basketball for New Heights, my staff and I are meticulous about acclimating young, excited youth to the game we love. We bring a healthy balance of Fun and Fundamentals to our weekend programming, and we introduce a quote or word of the day to teach positive affirmations to the young brothers and sisters we serve. Our goal is to empower our youth, nurturing a sense of confidence while teaching skills that come with the game.

In the past few years, the Jr. NBA has done a great job of introducing the game of basketball to different communities, by way of individual NBA franchises in their respective areas. I have worked for the Jr. Knicks and have been blessed to share the game with young boys and girls of all races, religions, denominations, and cultures. In my role with the Jr. Knicks, we used both basketball clinics and camps to introduce the fundamentals of the game, while also teaching values and character-building skills at the same time. The Jr. NBA philosophy "is to share the game of basketball with youth across the world by teaching skills, values, and wellness in a positive and fun environment."

It does not hurt that some of these clinics or camps have featured guest appearances by one of the current or former players of the Knicks team. The pictures taken and autographs signed are priceless to the youth who attend the events. Seeing the smiles on the children's faces has personally reminded me of the unconditional happiness the game brings.

THE NEXT PHASE OF INSTRUCTION

As your child becomes more advanced, it is time to go from the instructional phase to the competition stage. Here is where you must be more precise in choosing a coach. You know your son or daughter's personality. Do they need a coach who is going to push them hard, or do they need a coach who will have patience? As a parent, be real with yourself, as well. Are you looking for a coach or a babysitter?

I have witnessed many parents from my program leave their children with our developmental coach during practice and never ask him for feedback regarding their child's performance. My Brooklyn Bridge Basketball Smurf Program was made up of children between the ages of six to nine years old. Our Smurf instructor, Coach Avalon, was dedicated to his craft. He got up early every Saturday in the winter and left his own family, including his newborn, to devote time to children who wanted to learn how to play basketball. He has a pure passion and love for teaching and working with youth and he is just one example of selfless coaches that I know. So many other coaches in so many communities deserve our appreciation for their voluntary sacrifice. Their time is just as precious as the parents' time; therefore, the respect for time is a key component in this coach/parent/player relationship.

After cultivating the joy in our youth, the next phase of instruction that a coach must establish is to teach the fundamentals while sprinkling in team competition. Repetition is key when it comes to instruction. That's why your child's coach needs to establish boundaries and structure before he gets to the teaching part.

What does discipline look like? First and foremost, it starts with you as a parent being punctual. It is up to you to get your child to practice on time; be early if possible. The earlier your child is there, the better the chance she will be awake, alert and, hopefully, warmed up. Again, a good coach is a good teacher, and a good teacher is a good coach. So, she needs to make sure your child has their full attention when the whistle is blown.

A coach should never allow idle talking or walking in practice. Everything the coach says and every drill he does must be purposeful. He should be coaching from an already prepared practice plan; the coach should NOT be "freestyling" through his lesson plan. Many of the drills should be done with maximum intensity to simulate the speed of an actual game.

Coaches should correct all errors in a positive manner or, as I like to say, with P.E.A.C.E. which stands for POSITIVE EDUCATION ALWAYS CORRECTS ERRORS or POSITIVE ENERGY ALWAYS CREATES ELEVATION. I often use the P.E.A.C.E. acronym with my coaching staff and players. Both apply to the next phase of instruction. I believe that children should be pushed past their comfort zones with love.

"Positive reinforcement is a concept in behavioral psychology that can be used to help teach and strengthen behaviors. This process can be used as part of a formal training program, but it is also something that can occur naturally in everyday situations as well." (verywellmind.com)

If your child once struggled with a goal in a drill and now accomplishes it, it would be a good time for the coach to stop practice and reward him with a water break and some verbal encouragement before going to the next drill.

As we focus on the competitive phase of a child's development, I suggest parents make them understand that the most important person they will be in competition with is themselves. For example, children who do a certain number of push-ups on Monday should be aiming to increase that amount gradually. The more and the earlier she begins to embrace competing with herself, the easier the transition will be when contending with others.

I always looked inward for my competition. My mother told me to become the best version of myself. I have her motherly coaching encoded somewhere in my blood and I take that same approach with my players. It is my duty, with their permission, to pull the gold, diamonds, and other special treasures out of their psyche, while teaching my student athletes to have an unlimited vision for their lives. Ultimately, I want them to shine as bright as the sun on the court *and* off the court.

When the competitive phase of your child's development begins, hopefully you will have a coach who will put them in realistic situations. There is no need to put your child in an overwhelming environment. A child should be playing against equally matched competition until they or their team is ready to move on to the next level. As the legendary entrepreneur/rapper Nipsey Hussle once stated, "It's a marathon." The sports journey is certainly not a sprint.

There is not much good that can come out of your child's team getting consistently embarrassed by superpower teams. I have seen lopsided games of 50-3 in ten-and-under aged games. Sure, lessons can be taught by a game like that, it can be used as a way of getting your team's attention. I get it! However, losing like that consistently can also build bad habits, as well as a victim's attitude, especially in young athletes, which is not productive in sports or in life. On teams that lose consistently, morale often suffers.

On the other hand, if your child is on a good team that is advanced, they need to seek out the best competition, even if it is a year older than their age group. As your child gets better and their teams improve, they should never become satisfied with their comfort zone. He/she could gain a false sense of superiority in a sport if they are not challenged. Hence, they might think they are good but, in reality, not so much.

This is why travel teams are important. Travel teams provide the opportunity to compete against programs from different regions that play a different style than a player is used to seeing. Your child's team might be playing against opponents with an edge. A new style or a different skill will force them to make adjustments to their games. Or, your child's team might play against height and/or size they don't usually see in their town.

Always set your sights on the next challenge so you can continue to bring out the best in your child. In other words, your next move must always be your best move!!!

PEDOPHILIA IN YOUTH ENTERTAINMENT AND SPORTS

Unfortunately, there are inherent dangers in youth sports that people don't usually think about until it is too late. According to *Psychology Today*, The U.S. Centers for Disease Control and Prevention indicates the following:

"Pedophiles are often drawn to positive youth settings, such as schools, scouting, or sports, because such environments bring them into contact with so many potential targets."

Approximately one in four girls and one in six boys are sexually abused before the age of eighteen. Most victims suffer the abuse at the hands of someone they know, often a trusted adult.

One day, I watched the movie *Open Secret*, which documented childhood pedophilia in Hollywood. The movie highlighted youth entertainment managers in Hollywood who would assist children and their parents to get on commercials, television shows, or movies. However, these entertainment managers often used their influence to allow them to get close to children in order to perform acts of pedophilia.

Below are some risk factors from "Stop it Now!" that make a child vulnerable to sexual abuse:

- Weak or absent ongoing connection to a trusted, safe adult
- Child sees themselves as not deserving protection or
- respect

- Child feels emotionally isolated or neglected.

In the *Open Secret* documentary, Todd Bridges, a child star from the hit television show *Diff'rent Strokes* that I watched as a little boy claimed he was a victim of this assault on his sexuality. Actor Corey Feldman, who starred in *Gremlins*, *The Lost Boys*, and *The Goonies* movies, stated that this act of betrayal runs rampant in show business.

As I watched the documentary, I found in it a disturbing pattern that parents slowly relinquished control of their children to these managers after they took an interest in the children's career path. You may ask why I'm bringing this up. When I was growing up in New York City, Riverside Church's basketball program was haunted by strong rumors of pedophilia within their organization. As a child playing ball in New York, I would often hear gossip of Mr. Ernie Lorch's inappropriate behavior towards children. Ernie Lorch was a wealthy corporate lawyer and deacon at Riverside Church and was known commonly as the Godfather of AAU. Lorch helped launch the Riverside Church Hawks in 1961 as an outreach program for underprivileged kids.

His legendary Riverside Church basketball program was sponsored by Nike, and its alumni feature basketball legends such as Elton Brand, now the general manager of the Philadelphia 76ers, former NBA all-star Kenny Anderson, Hall of Famer Chris Mullin, former NBA star and current head coach of Long Island University Rod Strickland, and many more. Other less famous names would claim an association with Mr. Lorch as well. One person in particular, Robert Holmes, claimed Lorch sexually assaulted him and that he was paid hush money.

Holmes was awarded $325,000 in a court settlement, according to the NY *Daily News*.

"Several other men claimed they were abused as teens by Lorch, but the former coach was never charged criminally in New York because of statute of limitation issues. He was indicted by a

Massachusetts grand jury on attempted rape and indecent assault and battery of a person over 14 years old."

Lorch is now deceased but the scars from some of the trauma he caused are still alive.

When I coached in the Catholic High School Athletic Association (CHSAA), Christ the King High School traditionally had been one of the premier basketball programs in the league. They are ranked consistently among the top 50 basketball programs in the nation. Bob Oliva was the head coach of the boys' varsity team. He won 549 games and four CHSAA Class AS intersectional titles during 27 seasons at Christ the King and is in their Hall of Fame.

I played at Bishop Loughlin when Coach Oliva was the head coach of CTK and, later, coached against him as head coach. When I coached AAU, I sent Mr. Oliva an eighth- grade player, who he recruited from my Brooklyn Bridge Basketball program. I have been at many CHSAA league coaching meetings with him, and we have talked many times. Years later, I was shocked to see that he pleaded guilty to sexual abuse charges in Massachusetts. He was indicted by a Boston grand jury last year on two counts of rape of a child and faced two life sentences but will not serve any time in prison.

He acknowledged that he abused Jimmy Carlino during a trip to Boston in 1976. Mr. Carlino claimed in a lawsuit that Oliva abused him more than 100 times over a four-year period during the 1970s. Allen Watson, a former Christ the King student who, at one time, pitched for the Yankees and the Mets, stated Oliva showed him pornography, masturbated in front of him, and took him to prostitutes when he was a teenager. Mr. Watson stated, "Bob Oliva is a monster."

In Cedar Rapids, Iowa, an AAU coach named Greg Stephen of the Adidas-sponsored Barnstormers was sentenced to 180 years in federal prison after he was convicted for collecting sexual images of 440 boys and molesting more than a dozen boys in a twenty-year period.

More than 250 women and girls claim Dr. Larry Nasser, the former USA gymnastics team doctor and osteopathic physician at Michigan State University, had sexually abused them while employed as team physician. USA Olympics disciplined him in 2015, but some of his accusers claim they complained about his behavior as early as the 1990s.

Rachael Denhollander was the first gymnast to come forward at the tender age of fifteen. Many of the victims stated that Nasser was able to hide his conduct behind the institution of the Olympic Training Center, run by coaches Bela and Marta Karolyi. They were accused by some of managing and coaching these athletes in an "emotionally abusive environment." Mr. Nasser is now serving a life sentence in prison, while his courageous victims are scarred for life with the trauma that he left behind.

Jerry Sandusky was the assistant coach for Joe Paterno at Penn State. Coach Paterno has the record for the most wins as a football coach in NCAA Football Subdivision history. Sandusky founded The Second Mile, a non-profit charity serving Pennsylvania's underprivileged and at-risk youth. In 2011, following a two-year grand jury investigation, Sandusky was arrested and charged with 52 counts of sexual abuse of young boys over a fifteen-year period from 1994 to 2009. According to court testimony, Joe Paterno knew of Sandusky's abuse in 1976. However, Paterno claimed he did not know until 2001. A Pennsylvania judge eventually sentenced coach Jerry Sandusky to 30-60 years in prison.

All the sexual predators that I have mentioned seemed to have hidden behind their acts of charity and the prestigious institutions that provided them cover. For example, many brothers who have played for Mr. Lorch shared memories of his benevolence. However, they have also heard the rumors of his famous "paddle" he allegedly used on the backsides of young boys in his office.

John Manly, the lawyer who defended some of the gymnasts, stated,

"What Nasser did is come in with a sunny personality, I'm a nice man you can trust me, gave the kids candy, listened to their problems and they liked him, and they trusted him, and he used that trust to disguise sexual assault as medical treatment."[1]

At the time of this writing, New York Attorney General Letitia James is launching an investigation into allegations of sexual abuse from multiple students at Babylon High School in Long Island.

Some of the exposed and alleged assaults in sports prompted the Amateur Athletic Union to announce mandatory background screening for all staff, coaches, and volunteers and to create a new directive to address some of the problems in the youth sports culture. Former AAU president Louis Stout stated, "The new recommendations are not because we suspect anyone, but rather because we expect everyone to do their part to create a strong, new culture of safety."

Children who have been molested may develop dysfunctional relationship skills as adults. They may have difficulty with intimacy and may keep friends and romantic partners at a distance. Adult survivors are seven times more likely to abuse alcohol and drugs than individuals who were not molested, according to Darlene Barriere, a violence and abuse prevention educator.

The long-term effects of child assault can be disastrous. Therefore, we, who are in the village with our children, must be proactive. All of the protectors—parents, coaches, uncles, aunts, grandparents—must be vigilant. Nelson Mandela once noted, "Our children are our greatest treasure. They are our future. Those who abuse them tear at the fabric of our society and weaken our nation." We must protect our children with our lives. Thus, parents, must do the research. You might ask a prospective coach these questions:

Tell me about yourself.

---

[1] Janis, Linzie, Jesko, Jackie and Kessel, Michelle: "Former female gymnasts accuse doctor of molesting them during treatment." ABCNews.com. 24 Feb 2017.

Why do you want to work with children?

Where do you currently work?

Have you ever been arrested and why?

Where have you coached before?

How do you intend to build relationships with your

players?

What are your core values?

What is your approach to teaching the game?

These are only initial questions. The longer your child travels through the world of sports, it is up to you as a parent to stay vigilant, not only about sexual predators but about financial exploiters as well as other opportunists. The higher your child climbs up the ladder of success, the more you will need to insulate your child with people you trust.

Stay woke, especially if you begin to deal with someone who is taking a business interest in your child, such as an agent, financial planner, or business manager. Make sure you ask other parents about their experiences. It is up to you to do your due diligence with anyone who takes an interest in your child's life.

If you are a parent who is not comfortable asking hard questions, make sure you have someone in your circle, such as a coach, spouse, uncle, auntie, grandmother, or trusted confidant, who does not mind asking them. Whether it be an agent, financial planner, or future coach, it is your responsibility to determine what course of action your family will take.

CHAPTER 4

THE AMATEUR ATHLETIC UNION (AAU)

C hoosing an AAU Program Amateur Athletic Union (AAU) members are comprised of individual memberships of staff, coaches, and players, all of whom must buy a membership. AAU clubs or programs also have to register and pay for membership. There are different types of AAU programs that a parent can choose from; there is no cookie cutter approach to joining an AAU program.

All organizations do not provide the same services or have the same values. It is up to you to research programs to find the right fit for your child's needs. Some big-time players have come out of small, lesser-known AAU programs and have had successful careers. Tyrese Halliburton, a six-foot-five sophomore from Iowa State, who was drafted by the Sacramento Kings, and now plays for the Indiana Pacers, is known for his ability to shoot and make plays. He played for a local AAU program in Oshkosh, Wisconsin, even after he was recruited heavily to play with teams on one of the major sneaker circuits. He never left. Halliburton stated:

"I value relationships more than anything in this world. Coach Johnikin and the DeBakker family [the directors of Wisconsin United] put so much time in me that there's no way that I could leave them high and dry and leave that program and not follow through with it."[2]

As I discuss the different types of AAU programs, hopefully I can help guide you in your decision. My biggest advice in this process

---

[2] Jonathan Tjarks. "The NBA Draft's Most Polarizing Prospect Is a Walking Analytics Experiment." *The Ringer*. 27 Nov 2019

is that parents/guardians be realistic about their children's talent level. Self-knowledge is very important in this process.

In New York City, there seems to be an AAU basketball team on every corner. However, there are not as many AAU basketball *programs*. Programs are not teams; programs usually consist of many teams. An elite youth basketball organization provides services beyond just putting teams in tournaments. For example, New Heights Youth Inc., where I am a director, provides national basketball exposure for both boys and girls, as well as academic support, tutorial services and team building workshops.

Programs are usually defined by their culture. In many communities in NYC, there are teams that were put together the same week as the tournament's start and, sometimes, the same day. Community coaches of these teams serve as mentors and do a good job of occupying the kids in the summer. Without neighborhood coaches, many children might be participating in unproductive or self-destructive activities. Unfortunately, these random teams often lack discipline, structure, and chemistry. Usually, they are no match for a program that has teams that play year-round and practice multiple times per week.

As a coach, I never wanted to pick up children randomly and put them in a game. I always felt that was a no-win situation based on what I expected from players and what they anticipated from me as their leader. Even if I had to coach in an all-star game, I wanted to have a brief practice to get all the players on the same page and to be organized. Despite what one of my favorite players, Allen Iverson, expressed in his famous "practice" rant, I always thought proper preparation was a way of showing respect for the game. I wanted my program and teams to reflect the high level of honor for the game that I have—with good practices, training, and conditioning.

As a parent, you need to get the maximum out of the AAU program you are seeking for your son or daughter. The earlier you can get them acclimated to some of the demands of being a student-athlete, the better it will be for their future. The program you choose should serve as an extension of the values and principles you want to teach your child at home. I have seen very talented players come to my program but not stick because they could not handle our way of doing things. At an early age, some youth develop bad habits, such as showing up for games without attending practices. These kinds of players don't usually have the discipline to work on their game. Instead, they often get caught up in the early hype that comes from the hood.

Some coaches will tell their players how good they are and pamper them, without ever teaching accountability or advising them to put in the work to get better. These players quickly fall in love with being a "hood superstar." Unfortunately for many of these young athletes, the hood superstar title is sufficient. That mentality usually has an earlier-than-planned expiration date. When one person is not working, there is someone somewhere who is. That is a guarantee!

As a director and coach of a program, I strove hard to build a family-like culture. I understood that my Brooklyn Bridge Basketball program represented the same type of environment as a gang, but with positive motives, goals, values, and structure. It is well known that most of the influential elements of the street impact boys the most between elementary and middle school.

In our program, we wanted to show black boys, and boys of color, that they could find their mentors at "the Bridge." We sought to provide a positive platform for our youth, who we referred to often as "Young Kings." We prided ourselves in promoting brotherhood. Like a strong gang, we were aware that symbolism was important, so we "banged" for our uniform colors, which were black, silver and white.

My coaches and I were sincere with our visions for our young men; we wanted them to have the feeling that they were being looked after. Many of the young brothers did not have a father living in the home. Whether their father was in prison, dead, or did not reside in the same state, my coaches and I worked hard to fill the void. We were always conscious of our roles in these young men's lives.

We served as their fathers, uncles, big brothers, or just "big homies" and took our roles as mentors seriously. Our motto as coaches: "It's bigger than basketball!"

If a family-oriented environment is important to you as a parent, make sure you choose a program that offers a holistic approach to your child's development. Black children, in particular, can no longer be put in the limited "athlete" box. Our children are way bigger than any box. Therefore, if available, choose a program that offers more than athletics. Research to determine whether they offer academic support, mentoring, off-court group outings, and character-based training.

Lastly, your participation as a parent is very important, as important as it is in school. While simply showing up at your child's games is important, all good programs thrive due to the sweat equity that comes from parental involvement. What does that look like? Well, picture yourself carpooling, assisting with fundraising, tournament scheduling, organizing travel logistics, assisting with washing uniforms and so on. As a parent it does not matter what you do for the team, as long as you are making a positive contribution.

MIDDLE SCHOOL AAU

The middle school AAU circuit all over America has developed tremendously in the last 10 years. When I jumped back into the grassroots basketball culture after scouting full-time in the NBA for many years, I did not realize how intense and professional it had gotten. It has become a lucrative industry. For example, on the girl's circuit, the Rose Classic, founded by my friend Anton Marchand, has been the platform young ladies use to highlight their talents. Over the years, some of the best WNBA players have emerged from this tournament.

All three major sneaker companies have subcontracted out to private groups to run their middle school AAU circuits. Made Hoops, founded by Chad Babel, is the standard bearer for all middle school tournaments. It features many teams, such as the 2021 Nightrydas Elite and Each One Teach One, both out of Florida, that could easily beat a lot of high school teams. The 2021 Made Hoops Finale which was held in Augusta, Georgia, in July was won by the New York Lightning and some of the top eighth graders in the country including one standing at six-feet-eight inches. In 2022 I coached the New Heights 8th grade National team. We participated in the Made Finale. We went 3-0 in our pool before getting beat by DNA Elite from Virginia. Some of the best players at these tournaments have been "re-classed," which I will talk about later in the book. Some of the top ranked seventh and eighth grade prospects easily can be seen on this circuit showing their talents off for the top scouting services in the country to evaluate.

Under Armour has a Future circuit and Adidas has their Gauntlet circuit. Parents have become especially invested in this phase of the game because it can help young athletes get into good high schools. Savvy parents use middle school grassroots programs as a platform, no different from student-athletes using high school as a platform to get to college. It is all relative and just as intense.

In 2018, my Brooklyn Bridge Basketball sixth grade team finished as the runner-up in the championship of the Adidas Circuit. We were a team full of twelve-year-old and under players. We were overmatched in the championship against sixth graders from Philadelphia, who could have easily been in the seventh or eighth grade. On these circuits, you will certainly run into teams with children playing eighth grade basketball who are fifteen and sixteen years old.

On the grammar/middle school grassroots circuit, there are tournaments that have divisions that start children as early as eight years old. There are district tournaments that precede AAU national tournaments in every area. For example, the district championships in New York City are often held at the Island Garden facility in Long Island. The winner of the district championship gets placed as a number one seed in the national tournament. My twelve-and-under team accomplished this in 2018. Later, we went on to win the AAU national championship, led by head coach DeSean Gist, who was my point guard at Bishop Loughlin, and is now a coach on their varsity staff.

The national tournaments are played in select cities around the country. The AAU National Championships are well run and provide good competition. It allows children to play against teams from all over the country. The Nationals offer three different tiers of competition. Division I is for the top teams, and Divisions II and III are for the less advanced teams.

In the 2022 summer my eighth grade team won the United States Basketball Association USBA National Championship in Charleston, South Carolina, against Wisconsin Playground. We won seven games in a row to accomplish our ultimate goal. It was a great experience for my team. They were awarded with rings, medals, shirts, and hats.

In the next few years, middle school AAU basketball will become even more intense with the anticipation of high school players being able to go straight to the NBA again, which has been prohibited since the 2005 NBA draft. As the eighth-grade National coach for New Heights, I have driven to homes, made constant calls to parents and texts to players to get some of the top eighth graders in the region to play for my team. This process is no different than what is expected of an assistant coach at St. John's University, Georgetown, or Michigan State. In fact, one day some of these young men will be playing for these distinguished universities. That is their hope, at minimum, for their parents and for them. In the near future, NBA scouts as well as college coaches will have to be aware of players as early as seventh grade in order to gain an advantage against their competitors.

At the 2021 Nike Elite Youth Basketball League (EYBL) tournament NBA scouts were permitted to attend games and Coach John Calapari of the University of Kentucky attended an eighth-grade game. While I was at the games with my New Heights/Lightning high school teams, I was able to catch up with colleagues I had traveled with from such teams as the Washington Wizards, Detroit Pistons, Brooklyn Nets, and Indiana Pacers. The attention from NBA personnel will make the ranking process increasingly important. Inevitably, more money will flow into the middle school basketball scene; children and parents will increase their ambitions, and, unfortunately, corruption is bound to follow.

CHAPTER 5

THE RECLASSIFICATION FACTOR

I n approximately the last ten years, there has been a growing trend of young basketball players reclassifying in high school or before. Reclassification is a process where a player changes the date they were supposed to graduate from high school. If an athlete graduates from high school early but does not change the date he or she goes to college, there are rules that might impact his or her eligibility. The same goes for athletes who graduate on time from high school but delay their college enrollment.

While reclassification has traditionally pertained to high school athletes, reclassifying has now become popular on the junior high and even elementary school levels. In layman's terms, reclassifying is simply getting held back on purpose. Why would a parent allow their child to get left back? There could be multiple reasons.

AGE

There are many young athletes who, for whatever reason, started school early or, due to their academic prowess, were skipped a grade. Therefore, there are some kids entering ninth grade at thirteen years old, while on the flip side there are some kids entering ninth grade as old as fifteen and even sixteen years old. Needless to say, there is a big difference between the body size and intellectual maturity of a thirteen-year-old and a sixteen-year-old.

Thirteen-year-olds are more likely to have social esteem issues, to be very concerned with body image, convinced that everyone else is watching and judging them, uncertain, unhappy, sensitive, or withdrawn (*Greatschools.org*). They tend to spend a lot of time alone and need their privacy. Contrarily, fifteen- and sixteen-year-old children are starting to date and have relationships. Their friends are very important, and their relationship with their siblings may be better than their relationship with their parents.

While girls start puberty between the ages of eight and thirteen, typically boys go through puberty between the ages ten and fifteen. Therefore, there is an inherent physical, emotional, and intellectual advantage that a fifteen- or sixteen-year-old freshman has over the traditional thirteen- or fourteen-year-old freshman. Yet, this is the new reality in grassroots and high school basketball.

Reclassifying is a loophole that parents use to gain an advantage and many parents are now doing it just to give their children a fighting chance against stronger, more mature competition. For example, in AAU basketball, a player has to meet a specific age requirement for the entire year. An AAU year starts on August 31st. Therefore, if a child is playing twelve and under, he cannot turn thirteen years of age until after August 31st of the following year. In the AAU world, we call youth born after August 31st "late births." While having a late birth child might be an advantage on a coach's twelve and under roster, it could put the child at a disadvantage in high school when his competition is a fifteen-year-old freshman. Interestingly enough, this occurrence is more rampant actually in football than in basketball.

ACADEMICS

Parents of middle or elementary school children often cite academics as another reason to re-classify their children. They want a "do-over" of the grade their son or daughter completed due to a lack of classroom focus or inadequate teaching, and they might reclassify their child in another school altogether. Getting left back can be a stigma that children would prefer not to deal with in the same school. Understandably, they want to graduate with their same classmates. They don't want to be known as someone who is not smart or "slow."

This re-shuffling of the deck can only happen before an athlete gets to high school. According to high school eligibility rules, when a student enters high school or secondary school, he only gets four years to be a student-athlete.

MEETING YOUR GOALS

The end goal is simple: some parents re-classify their children because they feel it puts them one step closer to getting a college scholarship or becoming a professional. Some parents have already spent a considerable amount of money in the hopes of landing that elusive athletic scholarship or to make their child more marketable to elite universities, travel teams, personal skill coaches, and summer sports camps.

So why should parents worry about the expense of another year of grade school (even at a private or parochial school)? That might be an easy question or a simple issue for the parent who comes from money and who has resources; however, for many students in the "hood," their parents must seek free ways to reclassify. All over New York City and in my borough of Brooklyn there are public junior high schools that will reclassify children without a registration fee. Many student athletes and parents have used Our Savior Lutheran (OSL) in the Bronx to reclassify as well.

When I was a high school coach, I recruited Doron Lamb to come to my school in the fall of 2005; but, he reclassified before attending Our Savior New America in Long Island for a year. The next year, he came to Bishop Loughlin and played varsity for two years before transferring to Oak Hill Academy, where he became a McDonald's high school All-American. His goal was to play high level Division I basketball, which he did at the University of Kentucky under Coach John Calapari. They won a National Championship in 2012. That year, he was drafted in the second round by the Milwaukee Bucks. Ultimately, he and his family met their goal!

Other elite prospects are on a mission to ascend to the NBA as fast as possible. Many are beginning to forfeit their last year of high school to do one year as a freshman at the college that recruited them. For example, Marvin Bagley III was the nation's Number One high school recruit in the Class of 2018 before making his announcement to reclassify back to the Class of 2017. He played one year at Duke University before being drafted as the number two pick overall by the Sacramento Kings.

Coach Bill Self of the University of Kansas commented on the reclass trend: "I think a lot of them are thinking, I can get to the [NBA] a year faster." He went on to say, "I think some are thinking, if I can be a freshman in college with the access to training and that kind of stuff, would I be better off postponing that a year? I think in some situations, it's a very worthwhile thought."[3]

What is not mentioned is that some of these elite athletes are just going back to their original grade after reclassifying in middle school. These players are examples of this trend: Andre Drummond of the Chicago Bulls, the ninth pick of the 2012 NBA draft; Nerlens Noel of the New York Knicks, the sixth overall pick of the 2013 NBA draft; and Noah Vonleh, currently playing with the Boston Celtics, the ninth overall pick of the 2014 NBA draft. All have followed the same formula and have used the loopholes in the reclassification process as a means to an end.

All of the players above were drafted in the first round and were paid on a rookie scale contract. Rookie scale contracts are

---

[3] Jeff Borzello. "How reclassification fast-tracks top prospects to college and the NBA." ESPN. 24 Jul 2018.

guaranteed for the first four years, with team options for the third and fourth years. Both Vonleh and Drummond were set to get paid a little over $4 million for their first two years in the NBA. With that type of pay scale, you can see why re-classifying becomes a big part of the process. Prior to attending the University of Oregon, Francis Okoro stated, "I'm already eighteen. Why should I wait to graduate when I'm almost nineteen?" he asked. "You just look at it, you see some people still in high school, people are already nineteen, twenty. It still hurts you in the draft."

When I scouted in the NBA, my colleagues and I often drooled in our war room meetings over prospects who had what we termed as having potential or upside. The age of the player was a big factor. Often, we imagined how the broad shoulders and gangly arms could fill out in our workout and training program. When we drafted young guys, in particular, we were betting on a "home run" or triple instead of a base hit. It is common thinking in the minds of NBA decision-makers that an eighteen-year-old freshman is more attractive than a 21-year-old. This is the reason that college freshmen or "one-and-dones" are usually picked first in the NBA draft.

Analytics also played a part in our evaluation. It is commonly known that most NBA players peak at the age of 26 years of age. Sports economists David Berri and Rob Simmons explained how they "looked at the impact various factors have on NBA performance. Aging was one of those factors, and what [they] found is that player performance tends to peak around 26." Therefore, economically, NBA teams are getting more bang for their buck the younger they can get talent since they can pay their rookies on the rookie salary scale.

Often, I am asked how I feel about reclassifying. In my opinion, it depends on each individual and what the realistic goal is for your child. If you think your child needs to strengthen his academics and mature before he gets to high school, by all means reclassify. If you want your child to have a chance to compete physically because he is one or two years younger than kids from his class, I get it. If your child is a top 30 prospect in high school and you think another year of high school would hurt the strides she has made thus far— and that is your reason for reclassifying—I ask, why not?

My only advice is to be honest about your goals as you assist your child in the decision-making process. You will also want to work with industry experts to help you make a calculated choice. You will need to make sure your child has a plan and commits himself or herself to the game in that reclassification year. Student athletes need to hit the weight room, increase running to help with conditioning, and work on weaknesses. They will not get better automatically because they are older. Student athletes need to take full advantage of the time because they will not get it back. At the end of the day, the ends justify the means, like the prospects I mentioned in this chapter demonstrated in their careers. The overall game you are playing is chess, not checkers!

CHAPTER 6

CHOOSING A HIGH SCHOOL COACH/SCHOOL

C hoosing the right high school is one of the most critical decisions a parent and child can make together. Throughout my career, I have seen so many ways that parents have gotten this decision wrong. A lot of parents overthink it, but I have witnessed numerous parents who allow too many people into their circle who offer the wrong advice. A bad high school decision could result in you and your child having endless meetings with the coaching staff, due to a lack of playing time. It could also lead to your child failing because the academics are too rigorous. Usually, after disappointment sets in at a particular school, the child seeks to transfer. I have seen players go from one school to another due to dissatisfaction and unrealistic expectations. Ultimately, no coach or school will be perfect. Therefore, when choosing a high school coach or school, make sure your choices are based on sound judgment.

Below are key questions, both academic and athletic, that you might consider before choosing a coach and high school. I have broken the questions up into two different categories, academic and athletic.

ACADEMIC QUESTIONS

- Is this an accredited school?
- What is the graduation rate at the school?
- Does the school offer SAT prep?

- Does the school offer tutorial services?

- Does the cultural makeup of the administration and teaching staff resemble that of the student body?

- What is the school climate like?

- How many AP/advanced classes are offered?

- What are typical class sizes (or student/teacher ratios)?

- Does the school provide Special Education support?

ATHLETIC QUESTIONS

- Would the team's style of play fit your child's game?

- Who else are they recruiting to the team besides your son/daughter?

- Who will they be recruiting the year after your child enters the school?

- Is the interest mutual between your child and the coach?

- Will your child have time and room to expand their game as they get older?

- What ball players have been successful coming out of this program?

- How connected is the coach to colleges, all-star games, camps?

- If it is a private institution, do they have tuition assistance for your child? If so, how much? Half? Full?

- Do academics take priority over athletics?

- Is there strong community support for the sports program?

- How much time will be devoted to player development or skill improvement?

- How often can your child get in the gym to work on their individual game?

You and your child should write down some of these questions before visiting a high school. These questions can begin to help empower your child and make him understand his value. Never go into any situation blind; do your research. I do not know how many times players that I have coached or been acquainted with have told me they were going to a certain school but, when the fall came around, as Biggie Smalls once said, "It was all a dream!" Dot your I's and cross your T's.

My godson, KJ, had an early, disappointing high school experience. He was recruited in eighth grade by Stepinac High School. Over the last four years, Stepinac has won a New York State 'AA' Federation Championship, a New York State 'AA' Catholic State Championship, a New York Archdiocese 'AA' title, and has been nationally ranked. During that time, according to their website, fourteen student-athletes have gone on to play Division I, Division II, or Division III basketball. So, to make it plain, they are a "basketball factory." My godson is a solid, heady point guard; but, like his father and me, he is vertically challenged. When he made it past five-feet-eight, we were ready to celebrate!

In eighth grade, KJ was offered a partial academic scholarship to Stepinac, due to his academic achievements. His freshman class was very good and featured some long, athletic wing players. The problem was a lot of people played his position which made it hard for him to get playing time. He spent most of the year fighting for "minutes."

Like most players who come off the bench, his room for error was lower than the starters. It is not easy to go from starting most of your time in grammar and middle school to coming off the bench. Eventually, KJ transferred from Stepinac because he and his father could see the writing on the wall. Unfortunately, this is the reality that many will face if they do not do their research during the recruitment stage.

Student athletes have to understand that, if they are a rising ninth grader, they are not the only ones who are being recruited by the high school coach. As a parent, as much as you can, try to find out who the school is recruiting in the class that is coming behind you as well. It is up to the parent to find out where your child fits on the depth chart.

When I recruited as a high school coach, I always started out with a wide net. I "kissed all the babies," smiled at all the mothers, shook all the fathers' hands, and was politically savvy. Late in August, I would begin to focus on the rising eighth-grade players I really wanted. My staff and I would attend most of the games of the prospects we prioritized in the fall and winter, as well as throughout the spring.

Most elite high school programs have affiliations with AAU or grassroots organizations. Some might even have on staff a coach from an AAU program. The coach serves as a kind of babysitter for the AAU program, so that a relationship can be maintained with the prospect.

Ultimately, when you are choosing a high school and coach, make sure there is mutual interest and transparent communication. Like any good relationship, what makes it successful is mutual love and respect. The same is true for your relationship with the school of your choice.

LANCE STEPHENSON, AKA BORN READY

As the head coach of Bishop Loughlin High School, I never recruited a prospect as hard as I did the eventual NBA player, Lance Stephenson. I met Lance's father, nicknamed "Stretch," in Lance Jr.'s sixth grade year. He was introduced to me by Lincoln High School head coach

Dwayne "Tiny" Morton with whom I had worked previously as an Assistant Coach.

After seeing Lance play, I knew right away that he was special. What jumped out about his game was his "motor." He played harder than everyone on the floor. In fact, I thought he played angry for a twelve-year-old boy. Or, perhaps he played with a combination of both passion and hunger, which is often inherent in many ball players who grow up in poverty, as had Lance.

Lance, aka "Born Ready," grew up in the Coney Island section of Brooklyn where almost 25 percent of its residents live in poverty. Lance's grit on the court reflected the enormous amount of fight it would take for him to navigate through all the systemic obstacles that are present in the hood. He had a competitive edge that was unmatched in youth basketball.

I will never forget the time he played with my Brooklyn Bridge Basketball program in the citywide tournament in Queens, NY. I had substituted him out of the game and, instead of sitting on the bench and resting, his father motioned for him to do push ups, which he did until I put him back in the game five minutes later. In other tournaments, he dominated in the fourteen-and-under division as a twelve-year-old. In one tournament, he led our twelve and under team to a championship and finished with a triple-double.

My early relationship with Lance and his family gave me leverage when I began recruiting him to Bishop Loughlin. When he was in seventh grade, I made sure he played in the Adidas-sponsored Camp Next, the incubator platform for the legendary ABCD camp, also sponsored by Adidas. The ABCD camp featured the likes of Tracy McGrady, LeBron James, and the late, great Kobe Bryant.

After Lance dominated Camp Next, I convinced one of my mentors, Gary "Gee" Charles, AAU grassroots legend and founder of the NY Panthers program, to allow him to play on his high school travel team. Lance also played on the sixteen-and-under team for the Panthers. His best game was at the Bob Gibbons tournament in North Carolina, where we competed against a Philly team that featured the smooth "bucket getter" and eventual 2010 NBA rookie of the year, Tyreke Evans. In that game, which we won, Tyreke probably scored about 40 points while Lance had about 30 points, ten rebounds, and ten assists.

The NY Panthers high school traveling team also featured future NBA players Danny Green and Joakim Noah. We played in "major" tournaments, such as IS8 in Queens, NY, as well as in the Big Time tournament in Las Vegas. Lance thrived off the bench as a seventh grader in a seventeen-year-old and under tournament. By that time, his buzz was growing as fast as a New York minute. By the fall of his eighth-grade year, Lance made an announcement to all scouting publications that he would be attending Bishop Loughlin for high school.

Lance's decision gave my school a lot of buzz and credibility. I knew the basketball brand at our school would change overnight once he put on our purple and gold uniform. However, I also knew I had a long way to go to get this done because of three words: Lincoln High School.

Coney Island is best known for its amusement park, the enticing smell of franks and waffle fries at Nathan's Famous Hot Dog, as well as the Hot dog Eating Contest, held every Fourth of July. To the Brooklyn sports community, Coney Island was the home of some of the best basketball players to come out of New York City. Lincoln High School represented the official launching pad for those ballers. There have been numerous Division I basketball players who have emerged from Lincoln High School: Jamel Thomas, a former Providence College basketball star; former NBA star Stephon Marbury, aka 'Starbury,' who was picked fourth by the Milwaukee Bucks in the 1996 NBA draft; and his cousin and former NBA player, Sebastian Telfair. These three and others helped build Lincoln's winning tradition in New York City.

The Public School Athletic League (PSAL) championships were almost a given for Lincoln, which was led by head coach Bobby Hartstein during the Marbury era and then "Tiny" Morton in the Telfair era. The coaching staff set their sights on higher aspirations with NBA talent on their roster; therefore, winning the state basketball championship was the only goal!

Bishop Loughlin had a good reputation as a competitive team in what many experts believed was the greatest high school basketball league in the country. At that time, I had probably the best rising junior in the city, Devin Ebanks, who was selected later to play in the Jordan Brand Classic All-Star Game. He played two seasons at West Virginia before the Los Angeles Lakers drafted him in 2010 as the 43rd pick. As a Laker, Devin was a teammate of the late Kobe Bryant.

Our league featured highly ranked teams, such as Christ the King, Rice, and St. Raymond's. They were the usual headliners in the CHSAA league. My recruitment plan was simple: I spent the whole year catering to the needs of the Stephenson family. I wanted to make the Stephenson family as comfortable with me as possible. I also knew that Lance would still receive pressure from the Coney Island community to go to Lincoln.

I was no fool, but I dared anyway, against all the odds. At the same time I was maintaining my relationship with Lance, I was using his commitment and the publicity it generated for our program to lure two seventh grade phenoms, JayVaughn Pinkston and Doron Lamb. Pinkston would go on to play at Villanova, and Lamb went on to play at the University of Kentucky, winning a National Championship with current NBA superstar and Los Angeles Laker, Anthony Davis. Eventually, Stephenson, Pinkston, and Lamb became McDonald's All-Americans. These three players were my priority.

My recruiting philosophy was to go after all the players I thought would be big time. Then, I wanted my assistant coaches to go after the second-tier players. Why? Because I knew from my experience in the grassroots basketball world that elite players and their parents often need special attention. Their calls must be answered. At times, they will need rides to games. They will want to talk about attaining additional benefits for their son to attend a school, which could be anything from getting sneakers for their grandmothers to adding on a lunch expense to the tuition they would receive. I preferred that all those issues go through me.

Lance attended Bishop Loughlin's summer program, which was an orientation for incoming freshmen before the start of the school year. We stayed in contact throughout the summer, and we even had conversations with him about moving to the Clinton Hills section of Brooklyn where Bishop Loughlin is located. This move was meant to protect him from daily interrogation by people in his Coney Island community about why he was not going to Lincoln HS.

However, things took a turn for the worse. After playing in the Nike-sponsored local Conrad McRae tournament to close out the summer, Lance and his father had a meltdown in the park when the tournament awards were announced and Lance was not awarded the MVP. A bottle was thrown, and curse words were shouted. I tried to talk to Lance Sr. in the park to give him some insight and calm him down, but he was not willing to listen to me. I did not realize it at the time, but he would no longer be willing to adhere to any advice from me as he once had. Our relationship was never the same.

As usual, on the first day of school I went to welcome all the freshmen, only to find out that Lance was a no-show. My heart dropped. I knew that the platinum-hit record I was ready to play for the entire country had been remixed. One of my coaches said it best: it was like we were about to party and pop the champagne and someone knocked the bottle out of our hands. We had visions of Lance hoisting up championship trophies and pumping his fist in the air to the fans, as Michael Jordan once did for the Chicago Bulls. We were going to make the purple and gold colors the hottest colors in New York City.

All those dreams faded very quickly when we found out Lance decided to attend Lincoln High School. Just like that, whatever relationship I thought Lance and I had built evaporated. I received no heads-up phone call from the family, nor did they return any of my calls. Instead, I had to make a humbling call to Sonny Vaccaro, the grassroots basketball guru who supported my efforts in recruiting Lance, to tell him that Lance would not be attending my school anymore. His reply was short and to the point, "Ok, Khalid, so no uniforms." He was referring to the custom-made, Italian-designed uniforms that Loughlin would have been wearing had Lance been on the team. I was a coach with egg on my face.

Although the entire basketball world knew about my Lance Stephenson debacle, they would never get the satisfaction of seeing me look weak. I was raised to always stand with ten toes down as a soldier, regardless of how hard the winds blew. I kept a mean poker face, though I certainly was embarrassed and hurt. Like any good hustler, I had to bounce back quickly and move on to the next play. I charged the whole experience to the game and learned not to take it personally.

Overall, Lincoln's recruitment of Lance paid dividends for that institution. Lance led Lincoln to four straight PSAL championships and, in 2009, became the all-time high school scoring leader in New York State history. All the local and national news that Lance generated helped Lincoln receive free marketing and ultimately helped their overall student enrollment. Lincoln received an enormous amount of apparel from Adidas; they were invited to national tournaments, and they were recipients of resources that they would not have received without having had an elite player on their roster.

Lance went on to spend one year at the University of Cincinnati before being drafted by the Indiana Pacers as the 40th pick in the 2010 draft. Currently, Lance is playing again for the Indiana Pacers. I always rooted for him from afar and still do. I have seen him and his family many times since his decision to attend Lincoln, and we have remained cordial and respectful.

Like the grassroots world, high school sports are a lucrative business. Mark Conrad, associate professor of legal and ethical studies at Fordham University School of Business, called it "an economic juggernaut." In the summer of 2012, the New York City public school system negotiated a two-year, $500,000 contract with the MSG Varsity Network— a Cablevision network—to broadcast all types of high school athletic events.

ESPN regularly broadcasts high school football and basketball games now. I wrote this book in the middle of the COVID-19 pandemic. Because of social distancing requirements, live streaming of both AAU and high school games might be the norm in the future, for example, all the EYBL games (Nike circuit games are streamed on nikeeyb.com). Also, BallerTV.com, TheSUVTV.com and BeTheBeast.com stream many grassroots and national high school games. Inevitably, the money that flows into amateur sports will continue to increase exponentially. Hence, at the ground level, the recruitment of players who come with lucrative resources will become even more of a blood sport.

I share my Lance Stephenson story because, I want to give you an inside view of what recruiting a top talent looks like. I also went above and beyond to recruit a six-foot-four-inch guard when I first became head coach at Bishop Loughlin. I met this young brother at the ABCD camp. He was a strong, athletic guard who dunked the ball with ease. I was introduced to him by an agent friend. The young student-athlete was from Canada, and he was looking to play basketball in America. I was looking to start my tenure at Bishop Loughlin with a splash. Needless to say, the young man and I got on the same page very quickly. Now, he had to convince his family that he had found a great fit, and I would have to convince my father and stepmother that they should let him stay with them.

At this point, my dad was a basketball junkie, so he had no problem with the game plan. He was 100 percent supportive of all my career goals as a basketball coach; however, the talk with my stepmother would be the last part of the deal that had to get done. She was both jury and judge in this situation. To this day, I don't know what my father did or said to her, but he did his job. He got the job done!

Now I would have to find a way to get the young man to the U.S. without creating alarm. He did not have the proper paperwork to live in America. After much contemplation, I decided to drive to Canada to pick him up. I told him that he would have to pack lightly for when we crossed the border, in order to give the police the impression that we would be returning. When we got to the border, I was very nervous, but I kept a straight face. I answered all the questions with confidence.

I was so happy when we crossed from Canada to the U.S., that all I could envision was a city championship in my first year. I wish I could say that it all worked out like that; however, bad news would soon follow. The young man was ruled ineligible by the CHSAA because he played for his own high school the year before. I could have used a high school transfer portal back then similar to the new NCAA college transfer portal that exists today!

My Loughlin team would go on to lose by one point in the CHSAA semi-finals to the eventual city champion, St. Raymond's. Even now, I believe had the young Canadian been ruled eligible, we would have won the CHSAA championship.

Lance and the "kid from Canada" were recruited by all means necessary. Depending on the talent of your son or daughter, you should be able to gauge how much a coach really wants your child. You can measure your child's worth to the athletic program based on the coach's dealings with your family. When recruiting top-notch talent, a coach will go the whole nine yards to obtain a major asset for the program, as I certainly had done. Although Lance did not play for me at Bishop Loughlin, I absolutely have no regrets regarding how hard I recruited him.

CHAPTER 7

SPECIALTY SPORTS PROGRAMS
THE ACADEMY SCHOOLS

I n the 1992 Olympics, the U.S. was represented by the "Dream Team" which featured Hall of Famers Michael Jordan, Magic Johnson and Larry Bird. They dominated the international field, winning every game by an average of 44 points. In the finals, they beat Croatia, which was led by eventual NBA champion Toni Kukoc.

Talking about the international impact of the Dream Team, Michael Wilbon, an ESPN sports analyst, explained:

"It really lifted basketball . . . and it gave birth to international stars, who had nothing to do with those games in '92, but who took so much from it." More international players kept coming to the U.S. to play in the NBA every year, and it all began from watching the Dream Team. Hall of Fame basketball player Charles Barkley added, "I've talked to Parker, Nowitzki, and Ginóbili. Their first love of basketball started with the Dream Team, and I'm really proud of that."[4]

What cannot be ignored in recent years is the European basketball influence on America's school system, as it pertains to basketball. In Europe, youth players play for the same sport club year-round. Also, seasonally, players are taught by the same coach, which builds familiarity as well as continuity. European youth play under the umbrella of professional teams. The elite youth players are eventually groomed to play on their countries' summer national teams.

---

[4] Briley Perkins. "The '92 Dream Team: The Team that Changed the Game of Basketball Forever History Media." STMU Research Scholars. 6 Oct 2019.

NBA great and San Antonio Spurs legend Tony Parker is a product of an academy in France. He attended the esteemed National Institute of Sport, Expertise and Performance (INSEP) before playing professionally for the club Paris Racing Basket. Later, in 2001, he was selected in the first round of the NBA Draft by the San Antonio Spurs. Recently, he founded the Tony Parker Adéquat Academy in Lyon, France. The Academy will serve as both a training center for ASVEL's men's and women's teams, and an international school for students with the talent and aspiration to excel in specific fields, including basketball, eSports and music.

The NBA itself was once in talks about "creating academies that would house and train dozens of the country's elite high school basketball players," sources said. This academy concept has been floated for years, notably by Dallas Mavericks owner Mark Cuban. These academies would have been modeled after European-style operations that soccer and basketball franchises use and after the NBA's own international academies. Currently, the NBA operates three academies in China, one in India, one in Senegal, and has a global academy with prospects from across the planet at the Australia Institute of Sport. Recently, they opened another academy in Mexico City to serve standout Latin American teens.

The National Basketball Coaches Association has done a tremendous job recently of promoting the NBA's and the International Basketball Federation's (FIBA) "global basketball development and community outreach program that unites young basketball players to promote the sport and encourage positive social change in the areas of education, health, and wellness." Per the Basketball Without Borders website, "Camps have taken place in 13 cities and 11 countries on five continents."

Notable alumni of the Basketball Without Borders program include Joel Embiid, Pascal Siakam, and Danilo Gallinari. In 2019, the Rookie of the Year in the NBA was the sensational Luka

Doncic, born in Slovenia. In 2019 and 2020, the MVP of the NBA was Milwaukee Bucks superstar and 2021 MVP of the NBA Finals, Giannis Antetokounmpo, who was born in Greece to Nigerian parents. The latest MVP of the NBA was Serbian Nikola Jokic of the Denver Nuggets, which means the last three Most Valuable Players of the NBA have been foreign players.

In the 2021 summer Olympics, the roster of the USA basketball team included Kevin Durant, Damian Lillard and Jayson Tatum. Coached by Gregg Popovich, the team struggled in early international competition before winning the Olympic gold medal. At first, they lost two exhibition games against Nigeria and Australia. In the first round of pool play they lost to France. With access to talent every- where, it seems that the global sport of basketball is only going to get larger as the competition pool increases.

In 2018, I said on a podcast that if Africa had the AAU and high school basketball league structure that the U.S. has, they would eventually be the epicenter for the NBA's talent pool. I stated that you would have seven-footers at every position in high school. While the seven-footer at every position might be a stretch, I still believe that if the motherland had the resources and backing that America and Europe have, it would make the window to get into the NBA a lot smaller for athletes all over the world.

Recently, Former President Barack Obama joined NBA Africa as a strategic partner and minority owner. He is going to support programs that will focus on economic inclusion and his contributions will bring more validity to the African basketball culture. Also recently, Masai Ujiri, president of basketball operations for the Toronto Raptors and co-founder of Giants of Africa, committed to building 100 basketball courts on the continent.

During my years scouting in the NBA, I have had to travel to Canada on a couple of occasions to evaluate upcoming Canadian players in a suburb outside of Toronto at a facility called Athlete Institute Prep (AIP). AIP is a residential athletic training facility.

Their players attend a local public high school but play for Athlete Institute's basketball team. The facility offers structured workouts, nutritional plans, and physical therapy for their athletes to facilitate its robust game schedule. Notable alumni include rising NBA stars Jamal Murray and Thon Maker, who were selected seventh and tenth in the 2016 NBA draft, respectively.

As I walked around the facility, I saw what a standard institution for all aspiring athletes should look like. Immediately, I noted the disparity in modern technology and equipment between the Athlete Institute's and that of the U.S. high schools, especially in the inner cities. Hence, many parents, especially those of elite players, want to send their sons or daughters to what I describe as "basketball factories" or academies. Institutions such as Findley Prep in Nevada, Montverde Academy in Central Florida, Oak Hill Academy in Virginia, The Patrick School in New Jersey, St. Benedict's Preparatory School in New Jersey, and IMG Academy in Bradenton, Florida, are all sports powerhouses that pride themselves on developing their players, while keeping them away from the normal distractions of the inner city, from where many of today's elite athletes come.

Kanye West has gotten into the Academy School game; he built his Donda Academy, a private school for kids K-12 with only 60 students. They have received commitments already from Jahki Howard, a five-star prospect from Norcross, GA. Also, the New York Renaissance EYBL program recently opened a Charter School in the Bronx, New York, named after New York Knicks legend and Hall of Famer Earl Monroe. The school will focus on sports business but, inevitably, it will also be a nice landing spot for some of the top talent in the east coast region.

The National Interscholastic Basketball Conference is a new league that started in 2021-2022 and features some of the top Basketball programs in the country including La Lumiere School (Indiana), Sunrise Christian Academy (Kansas), Long Island Lutheran (New York), Montverde Academy (Florida), Oak Hill Academy (Virginia),

AZ Compass Prep (Arizona), Legacy (South Carolina), Bishop Walsh School (Maryland), Wastatch Academy (Utah), IMG (Florida). Their games are shown on various ESPN networks. Two of our players from the New Heights program played in that league for the Bishop Walsh School in Maryland.

Overtime Elite (Atlanta) offers top prospects between the ages of sixteen and eighteen years old a new pathway to the NBA. They offer an education as well as a six-figure salary. Their so-called amateur status would be forfeited, and the players would be able to make money off their names, images, and likenesses, among other things. NBA superstars like Carmelo Anthony, Kevin Durant and Trae Young of the Atlanta Hawks are investors in the league. One of my mentors, the former head coach of DePaul University and the University of Virginia (Dave Leitao), is an assistant coach of the Overtime Elite team.

A few years ago, I went to Florida to scout Anfernee Tyrik Simons, who played for IMG. He was selected later as the Portland Trailblazers' 24th pick in the 2018 NBA draft. As much as I was impressed by Anfernee's game, I was really blown away by the campus and facilities at IMG. On their website it states that they have "The World's Most Dedicated Student Athletes."

IMG's campus was just as big as some small colleges I have visited. For a young athlete, they have everything necessary for development, including four state of the art basketball courts, a wellness spa, and a golf course. IMG has partnered with ACP Sports Rehabilitation, "which provides IMG Academy training rooms with the same medical technology and advanced therapy programs that professional athletic trainers rely on in many college and pro sports teams, including those in the NFL, MLB, NBA, and NHL." (IMG Academy website)

Many elite athletes go to IMG to do their pre-draft training in almost all sports. IMG was a big player in the game of tennis before they developed their name in basketball and other sports. They have produced tennis stars, such as Maria Sharapova, and up and coming tennis star Whitney Osuigwe who stated:

"It's been so amazing at IMG," "I've worked with almost every coach here, whether it's the nutritionists, strength coaches, physios, tennis coaches or schoolteachers, and they all support me in so many different ways, as well as my family." (IMG Academy website)

This sounds like the same services that are offered when athletes sign with sports agencies. Hmm . . . .

In 2019, the IMG National basketball team won the GEICO High School National Championship. I attended the game, and the athleticism and strength of some of the athletes mirrored what I saw on some college teams. You could tell these young men were working out religiously in the gym, not just doing push-ups and sit-ups! Regarding their National Team, the IMG website states,

"IMG's National Team competes against some of the nation's top programs, while earning unparalleled exposure during showcases and nationally-televised games and tournaments. Student-athletes within the teams aspire to compete for top D1 programs or at the NBA and professional levels. Training consists of intensive workouts and team development that mirrors that of an elite collegiate program."

I received a call recently from one of the staff members at IMG asking my opinion of a player I had coached against in the New York/New Jersey area. The kid was only in the eighth grade. I said he was probably the best talent in this area, and I thought he had tremendous upside due to his length and skill. After all, the boy was about six-feet-four and could handle and shoot the ball with ease.

A week later the young man posted on his social media outlets that he would be attending IMG in the fall. He and his parents were eager obviously to take full advantage of all the resources IMG has to offer, and I can't knock them. For many young men and women, the traditional high school has become the dinosaur in the game; hence, high schools have become the feeding grounds for academy and prep schools. Many elite youths are using high schools as a temporary platform to get to play eventually at the Academy Schools where the resources, exposure and facilities are a lot better. The academies represent the new wave or, to be frank, semi-pro institutions of high school basketball.

ELITE GRASSROOTS PROGRAMS

Elite grassroots programs are sponsored by sneaker companies: Nike, Adidas, and Under Armour. Examples of elite grassroots programs in New York City include the PSA Cardinals program—sponsored by Nike—and New Heights, which was once sponsored by Under Armour and is now sponsored by Nike. After our merger with the NY Lightning, our elite high school program is now called New Heights/Lightning. The Atlanta Celtics have been sponsored by Adidas for as long as I can remember, and so have the Compton Magic of Los Angeles, to name a few programs.

In 2003, our NY Panthers had Joakim Noah, Danny Green, and Lance Stephenson on our roster. The Atlanta Celtics featured a frontline of Dwight Howard, Josh Smith, and Randolph Morris. Yes, they had two seven-footers and a wing who, in high school, could jump out of the gym. The Nike Mean Streets Grassroots program in Chicago was once backed by Adidas and featured a backcourt that consisted of former NBA MVP Derek Rose of the New York Knicks and Eric Gordon, who plays currently for the Houston Rockets.

Why are billion-dollar sneaker companies investing so much money in youth basketball? It is considered seed money, and the resources are used to build early relationships with potential clients. It is a corporate game played for long-term partnerships. When I was a student at Morehouse College, big corporations, such as Coca-Cola and IBM, plucked some of our "talented tenth" for summer internships. W.E.B. Dubois, the late Black civil rights and Pan Africanist activist, once coined the term "talented tenth" to describe elite intellectuals of the Black college educated. Those internships would lead often to long-term careers. Of course, initially these young men were going to be making copies and delivering coffee, not dunking basketballs. However, corporations in sports entertainment, as well as in other industries, traditionally form early relationships for financial gain by ingratiating themselves with the most talented of our community at the earliest ages possible.

No athlete and sneaker company has benefited more from their marketing relationship than Michael Jordan and Nike. It has been documented that, initially, Michael wanted to sign with Adidas, but they were not willing to give him his own signature shoe. I wonder where the guy who made that decision is now?

Michael Jordan signed his first deal with Nike in 1984. His contract was worth $500,000 per year and he received

25% in royalties. The original Air Jordan sneaker was released that year and became an instant hit, generating more than $100 million in sales in the twelve months after its release. Jordan has earned $1.3 billion from his Nike deal since 1984, including $130 million during the 2020 year alone, according to *Forbes* magazine. Since the inception of Jordan's hit sneaker, there has been an absolute frenzy by sneaker companies to find "the next one."

This motivation to gain financially has trickled down to AAU and high school programs, coaches, parents, and 'handlers' who, often, are chasing crumbs left by the corporations. The bigger the pie, the more everyone can share in the feast. For example, Tracy McGrady, aka T-Mac, the seven-time All-NBA selection and two-time NBA scoring champion, signed his Adidas contract out of high school for $1.7 million. The contract also had a provision in it for his high school coach to get paid $150,000 a year for six years. Yes, there are "bags" (money) out there for the best of the best!

I served as an assistant coach at Lincoln High School and co-director of the Juice All-Stars AAU program that featured the New

York City phenom point guard Sebastian Telfair. In 2004, Sebastian was awarded a $15 million sneaker contract. That relationship with Adidas was fostered at the ABCD camp. ABCD, which existed from 1984 to 2007, was an elite showcase for high school basketball stand-outs. The camp was the "Bentley Sedan" of basketball camps; they treated the players, coaches, and staff first class.

After some of my players were invited to participate, I worked at the camp with the rest of my high school coaching staff. The camp was held in East Rutherford, New Jersey, and the games were played on the campus of Farleigh Dickinson University. All players and staff stayed at a nearby hotel, which had a players' lounge equipped with video games and free after-dinner snacks. Every single meal— break-fast, lunch, and dinner—featured menu items that to this day still leave my mouth watering. All players and coaches dined together in a big reception room in the hotel.

The games were played after the morning session and featured some of the best young players from the country and the world. They would compete in front of the top college coaches in the country, including Duke's former head coach Mike Krzyzewski, Syracuse's Jim Boeheim, West Virginia's Bob Huggins, and many more. You name them, and they were there.

The camp existed during the era when players could enter the NBA draft out of high school. NBA scouts also worked at the camp as head coaches of the teams on which these prospects played. Hence, for a week, they were able to evaluate future NBA stars who participated at the camp, including Kobe Bryant, LeBron James, Tracy McGrady, Dwight Howard and others. This camp was a marketing jewel for the Adidas brand. The bells and whistles that came with the camp made it "the greatest show on earth" and a launching pad for many young hoopers of that era.

Adidas first formed a relationship with Sebastian Telfair when he was in eighth grade. Adidas spokesman Tony Gonzalez stated, "In getting to know him, we saw a charisma that made him someone we wanted to represent us. When you look at the ten or so high school players entering the draft, and you see the way he has handled the media, we felt Sebastian was that guy."

Years later, in 2019, Zion Williamson received a contract with Jordan Brand that extends five years and is worth $75 million, the richest annual rookie shoe deal in NBA history. After the signing, Michael Jordan said, "Zion's incredible determination, character and play are inspiring. He's an essential part of the new talent that will help lead the brand into the future."[5]

Similar to Telfair, this relationship originated with Zion and his family long before he signed the contract. Again, the first seeds planted in the race for Zion's services came through the grassroots basketball world. The sneaker company and its representatives used their brand to get a leg up on their competition.

Thus, the grassroots system serves as a platform for the recruitment of the best basketball players in the world, which tends to create a cutthroat dynamic. Grassroots directors, as well as coaches of elite teams, in turn need to attract players to maintain their resources or obtain more operational assets, which include sneakers, athletic gear (from head to toe), and travel money. It is no wonder that directors and coaches recruit against each other relentlessly to attract the best talent possible to impress the sneaker companies.

Nike has had the largest number of NBA players compete in their Elite Youth Basketball League (EYBL). For example, on the 2021 EYBL circuit, many of the top ranked players in the country competed and included the number one and two players in the class of 2021, Emoni Bates and Jalen Duren. Both played as freshmen for head coach and NBA legend Penny Hardaway at the University of Memphis. Emoni has since transferred to Eastern Michigan and Jalen was drafted with the 13th pick in the first round by the Detroit Pistons.

---

[5] Adam Zagoria. "Zion Williamson Signs Multiyear Deal with Jordan Brand." *Forbes*. 23 July 2019.

Under Armour and Adidas have national circuits also, but they do not have the cache of the EYBL. Therefore, if your child is not a mid-to-high Division I prospect, it is likely he/she will not make one of the existing Nike teams in your area. In fact, roster spots, which usually have no more than ten on a team, will be limited. Most of these programs have ninth, tenth and eleventh grade teams. Each level is more difficult based on the improved athleticism and basketball IQ of the competition. Participation on one of the lower teams absolutely will not guarantee a roster spot on the eleventh-grade roster. This is the most important and visible team in the program because that group is being scrutinized the most by sports writers, ranking gurus, sneaker reps, college coaches and NBA scouts. Ultimately, your child might get more playing time on the Adidas or Under Armour teams since they are not likely to be as talent-rich, yet they are still highly competitive.

Some of these grassroots programs start with teams at the fifth-grade level and continue up to the high school level. Similar to that of sneaker companies, the reason some programs start so early is a desire to cultivate a relationship with the young talent and their parents. Often, this gives young players who have history with a particular program an edge when they are older over players who try out for the team and do not have the same long-term connection.

Other grassroots programs find creating younger teams to be a waste of resources and would rather poach a player from another program once that player reaches eighth or ninth grade. They are not invested in the development process because some lack quality coaches. However, they do have plenty of handlers and recruiters who are looking for ready-made players.

The eighth-grade year of middle school is when recruitment and the attention of elite players intensifies. Grassroots programs are looking for The Next One to put on their platform. There may even be package deals, where savvy parents and players make sure they form alliances with the main player a program is recruiting to secure a spot for themselves. Towards the end of the eighth-grade season which ends in mid-August parents of top eighth graders are receiving recruiting pitches from grassroots coaches. Smart parents and players are weighing their options and doing their best to make the right decisions for their child.

Ultimately, when choosing a program to play for, whether it be AAU, high school, or college, remember this: playing time is the most important factor. College coaches do not care about your association with a high-profile team if you are not playing. They simply care about being able to assess a player's game on the court and against other competition. Clapping from the bench and handing out water is definitely a good gesture as a teammate, but it will not get your child the attention he needs to get recruited by a college coach.

Second tier AAU programs usually do not command sneaker deals. However, they might have the capacity to raise money or have a sponsor to assist with the expenses it takes to run a program. For this reason, these organizations do not travel extensively like the elite programs. On the East Coast, in particular, they might play on the Hoop Group or Zero Gravity tournament circuit. My New Heights program features high school teams filled with good players that could not make our EYBL teams but are good enough to compete at the tournaments I mentioned earlier. In many cases, second- tier programs serve as feeders for elite programs which often exploit the lack of resources of second-tier programs in order to entice talented players to jump ship.

When I was coaching with the NY Panthers, who at the time were sponsored by Adidas, I kept a close eye on middle school AAU programs. My pitch to young middle school players and their parents was that they could "play up" with our fifteen-year-old and under team. For an eighth grader who was dominating his own age group, I knew the challenge of playing up an age level or two was usually seductive. My ultimate goal was to get a prospect to play full-time with our program once he reached high school. I used this recruiting technique successfully with Sylvan Landsberg, who became a McDonald's All-American in 2008 and eventually played for the University of Virginia. He is now playing overseas.

In the recruiting game, I have been both the predator and the prey. I know from experience that when a staff member from an elite program recruits a kid who plays with a second-tier or unsponsored program, the outcome is usually a case of "big bank taking little bank." With that said, the second-tier program is a great fit for many youths. It keeps them playing the sport they love while they nurture long-lasting relationships. These programs also keep kids off the street with a focus on doing something productive.

It is not impossible for your child to get exposure in these programs, but it can be challenging. Why? Because college coaches are afforded limited time by the NCAA to evaluate players. The tournaments or games they attend must be "NCAA certified events." Usually, these official events are invite-only venues; most second-tier programs will not be summoned. Ultimately, some deserving children will not get to play on a platform sufficient to be seen by all college coaches. Unfortunately, grassroots basketball is a microcosm of America—a system of the haves and have nots.

WHEN THE HIGH SCHOOL PLAYER ACCOLADES COME ... OR DON'T

Almost every high school prospect wants to be considered one of the best. However, it is important to understand that there are levels to this. The journey to becoming an elite player is a marathon, not a sprint. Most athletes want to get to the NBA, NFL, WNBA, or MLB. I understand.

There may be early indications that a player might be on his/ her way, yet those are just early signs. A young player might be highly ranked in his class and might get invited to certain camps, tournaments, or teams, but that is no guarantee of ultimate success. For example, in grassroots basketball, elite players get invited to events such as the NBPA Top 100 camp, USA basketball camps and competitions, Pangos All-American camp, CP3 camp, the John Lucas Elite Invitational camps, as well as to specialized events run by Nike, Under Armour, and Adidas. These players may also get invited to elite showcase events, such as the McDonald's All-American, Allen Iverson Classic and Jordan Brand games.

In every event mentioned, there will be a few players who should have been invited but were not. The opposite is also true: there will be prospects who probably should not have been selected but somehow ended up in the showcase. If you were snubbed from one of those elite events, simply use it as motivation to get better. Let the rejection fuel your fire.

I remember scouting Montrezl Harrell in the Jordan Regional Game in 2012. At the time, he was ranked 90th in the ESPN class of 100. He finished that game with 22 points, twelve rebounds, and seven blocks. He was impressive and he displayed the same motor that he plays with today for the Philadelphia 76ers in the NBA. His "go-getta" mentality won him the Sixth Man of the Year honor in 2020. In my scouting report, I wrote that he was an "undersized four-man, but he plays bigger than his size." I thought *he had a chance*, as we say in the world of NBA when evaluating players who we believe can be successful professional players with the right guidance. After getting drafted in the second round by the Houston Rockets, it turns out he is making a great career for himself.

On the other hand, Anthony Bennett, in that same class as Harrell, was ranked seventh in high school. In 2013, he was chosen with the number one pick in the NBA Draft by the Cleveland Cavaliers. Years later, I watched him in the HSS (Hospital for Special Surgery) Brooklyn Nets practice facility. Along with many other former NBA players, Anthony was competing to make a roster spot during the free agent workouts we hosted. Days after the event, we cut him. I wondered if he ever loved the game. I thought he lacked what Harrell had naturally—a motor and a hunger. Bennett is known currently by many experts as one of the biggest busts in NBA history.

These two players' careers started off differently and are obviously on different journeys. Both have had to humble themselves at some point and, also, have been humbled by the game. Recently, I have seen a toxic level of arrogance in players from eighth grade through high school. It is not easy for children to deal with the accolades, social media hype, and attention they get as they succeed. When children do not stay grounded, centered, or have people around to keep them balanced, often they fall hard and fast without a safety net. The game can be cold for athletes who don't remain coachable and who have a poor work ethic. Regardless of how great any athlete becomes, humility is always required.

CHAPTER 8

COACHING FROM THE SIDELINES

Recently, I went to a pre-screening of the movie *King Richard*, the inspirational movie based on the life of Richard Williams, the father of Venus and Serena Williams and the architect of their Hall of Fame tennis careers. Richard and his wife went to great lengths to make sure their children could fulfill their destinies. He empowered them to have the grandest vision for themselves while planting deep seeds of confidence in their psyches. As I watched the movie, I could not stop thinking about Lavar Ball, who boldly predicted once that both of his sons, Lonzo Ball (Chicago Bulls) and LaMelo Ball (Charlotte Hornets), would be playing in the NBA when, at that time, they were amateur status.

I commend all parents for investing time, energy, and resources in their children. I have seen, firsthand, single mothers juggling the needs of all their children while still showing up to each of their child's AAU games. I have been proud to see so many Black fathers get up early in the morning to make their sons or daughters run, work out, or shoot 300 jump shots. These actions dispel the socially constructed myth that black men are not involved in their children's lives. The time and effort that these parents give is the sign of the commitment and love that will prove to be priceless for their child for years to come. Often, it also helps to nurture the bond between parent and child.

To the many grassroots and youth coaches all over the world, I respect and appreciate the time you spend molding, motivating, and teaching young children the many values that can be taught via sports. It is very important that parents express appreciation to coaches as well. I have had many conversations with coaches who say they only hear from parents when they complain. A simple acknowledgment or "thank you" goes a long way.

I still feel great when I reflect on a particular gesture of a father from our program who brought ice cold water to a game where we were playing in the hot August sun. I also remember the large smile one of the coaches in my program had after receiving an appreciation card with $100 inside from a mother when the season concluded.

Most youth coaches don't get paid a salary; at best they get a stipend. This does not truly compensate them for all the time they spend with children. Often, they use their own resources to provide gas and food after practice and games, as well as detergent to wash uniforms. Coaches put enormous numbers of miles on their cars, and they invest sweat equity with countless private motivational talks. Most coaches, like myself, have done all these things without any regret. We love teaching and we want to share some of the principles and values we have learned from the game with the next generation. The incentive is to pay it forward.

The relationship between a parent and a coach often can be complex; therefore, there needs to be an initial conversation regarding expectations and goals. It needs to be expressed that both coach and parent want what is best for the child. In my many years of coaching, I have come to realize that the parent, often exclusively, views the game from the lens of their child. The coach, on the other hand, is seeing the game from the lens of the team. Both perspectives deserve respect and attention; however, the most important dynamic in this relationship is honesty and transparent communications.

Make sure there are comparable expectations regarding your child's role on the team. If at any time you have a problem or conflict with your coach, seek them out for a private conversation. Give the coach an ample amount of time after the game to debrief. Listen to the coach's feedback on your child's performance with an open mind. I find it very immature for a parent or a coach to publicly bash each other after a disagreement, when often things can be worked out in a civilized fashion without the drama. Social media SHOULD NOT be the platform to express negative emotions. The public airing of grievances will do more harm than good for all parties involved.

Many parents I know have invested a whole lot of blood, sweat, and tears in sports with their children beginning as early as when they are six years old. It is a joy to see the bond that can be formed through the game of basketball. Like my own dad did with me when I was in high school, a lot of these parents invest time with their children by helping them with their jump shots, lay ups, and ball handling skills. They push their daughters to run an extra two laps or do ten more sit-ups. These parents rub the aching shoulders and knees of their children after a long AAU weekend. They stay up late showing videos of legends such as Shaquille O'Neal, Kobe Bryant, Cheryl Miller, and Sheryl Swoopes as a means of teaching the game. The investment made in their child's life is priceless.

In youth sports, parents need to refrain from coaching their child, particularly from the sidelines. In the game, your child's coach MUST be the primary voice that she listens to. If that boundary does not exist, a child will often look for a parent's approval or listen for their voice in the stands. This can be counterproductive to the coach's and team's agenda.

One day, when my godson KJ was playing in the legendary Conrad McCrae tournament in Brooklyn in the ten-year-old and under division, his father rode him the entire game. Every move he made was under a microscope and it was hurting his play, as he was playing tight. I had to tell his father, Khalil, to back off and let him play. I simply said, "Let him have fun and play loose." Khalil understood where I was coming from. He told me at the next game he could see the difference. I was able to make the point that it is hard to have a good feel for the game and use your natural instincts when you are also overthinking. In his article, "Why Parents Must Stop Coaching from the Sideline," Coach Mac states,

"Before the game and during time-outs, the coach will talk to the team about strategy and may give each player specific instructions to give the best chance of success. And then soon as a player gets out on the court, parents start screaming out conflicting instructions that go against the team's strategy and the player's role on the team. This leads the child in a tricky situation."

My point exactly! This type of parental behavior is a way of dividing and conquering the relationship between a young player and coach. In my experience, this not only causes tension between the coach, player, and parent, but it also creates a sense of chaos among the rest of the team. This only puts more pressure on a child to make the right pass, make free throws, or to execute the right play. I have seen children become outcasts among their teammates because of the resentment that is built up over time thanks to an intrusive parent.

As a coach, I have done my best to separate the transgressions of the parent and the sins of a player. However, if a child is not listening to my voice and command and, instead, is focused on what his parent is screaming, it will cost him. A head coach should not compromise his or her authority. If a parent does not have the trust and discipline to allow their child to be coached by someone else for the good of the team, then the parent should create a team of their own.

There is another kind of parental coaching that causes problems. I call it *covert coaching*, which is directed solely at the child based on a self-centered agenda. This hidden agenda rarely benefits the team as a whole. Parents who partake in covert coaching are just as harmful to the team as those who overtly coach from the sidelines. For example, if your child is knocking down certain jump shots in practice, I will have no problem with him shooting the same shot in an actual game. Contrarily, if he is consistently bricking jump shots in practices, I will not want him shooting those jump shots in games.

As a seasoned coach, I can sense when covert meetings have taken place. It is often manifested in children playing out of character and doing things in a game that they have not consistently shown they can do. Hence, the version of the child's game in the parent's mind and what the coach actually witnesses are at war!

For this reason, when coaching high school or AAU, I always like for my players to travel in the same vehicle to and from games. If we are on the road, I want them to stay in rooms with their teammates and not with their parents. When we dine at a restaurant, I want my players to sit together. This is to develop a team bond and allow my players to get to know each other off the court. In other words, I want to stimulate a brotherhood that will be as special as the bond the player has with their parents. When parents understand not to get in the way of that process, they are allowing their children to grow up and figure things out themselves, which they will inevitably have to do in life.

CHAPTER 9

THE BLACK STUDENT ATHLETE

The term student-athlete often is thrown around like a meaningless phrase in amateur sports. In theory, being a student matters; yet, actually, it lacks substance at many institutions. I have worked with young black boys in New York City, which has the largest school system in the U.S. I have noticed an absence of passion and purpose among young athletes as it pertains to academia. Sports are often used as the "carrot" that can be taken away if children lose their academic focus or, even worse, begin to fail.

Bishop Loughlin is a Catholic high school; however, I recruited most of my incoming freshmen from public schools. Thus, they often faced culture shock and were forced to make adjustments to a new setting. Not only were they expected to act differently compared to their public school culture, but many were also placed on academic probation for failing classes in their first semester. Even the freshmen who received good grades in junior high school struggled to get acclimated to the academic rigor and climate in Catholic school.

When one of the best players from my Brooklyn Bridge Basketball program was recruited by a coach to attend The Lawrenceville School in New Jersey, a private boarding school with tuition and fees per year currently set at $69,420, I took the drive with the player's family to visit the school. We were ecstatic about the opportunity that was presented. He was an A and B student at his public school in Brooklyn, so I was confident that he would do well on the Secondary School Admission Test (SSAT), which is a required entrance exam at many independent schools throughout the United States. He had to take this test to get into Lawrenceville. He did not do well on the test. But, I still felt that he should have been given a chance because of his character and work ethic. I did not feel it was right that this one opportunity came down to a single test.

The SSAT's own website refers to the test as, "The gold-standard test that helps students stand out in the admission process." Needless to say, my player, his family, and I were all extremely disappointed when the coach called and said that he could not get in based on his test scores. What we did not take into account at the time was that these tests are racially biased in favor of white American children. The internal bias of these tests has motivated The Association of Black Psychologists to call for a moratorium on the administration of IQ tests to black children, charging such tests:

Label black children as uneducable

Place black children in special classes

Potentiate inferior education

Assign black children to lower educational tracks than whites

Deny black children higher education opportunities

Destroy positive growth in and development of black children

In 1916, Lewis Terman, a known eugenicist who once served as President of the American Psychological Association, released the Stanford Revision of the Binet-Simon Scale, an individually administered intelligence test. "What he found was that his high IQ subjects (which he referred to as "Termites") tended to be healthier, taller, and more socially adapted than other kids. Based on his results, Terman suggested that gifted children should be identified early, offered tailored instruction, and have access to specially-trained teachers."[6]

---

[6] Kendra Cherry. "How Lewis Terman Influenced the field of Psychology." *Verywellmind.com.* 4 Apr 2020.

Hence, the architect of specialized tests had an agenda that was never meant to include black and brown students and, in 2021, those tests still don't.

When speaking about the SAT, the father of the SSAT, Monty Neil, the deputy director of Fair Test, stated that schools rely too heavily on the SAT in admission decisions. One test, he said, is not the best predictor of college success. "In a technical sense, it's probably not a biased test. The problem becomes in how it gets used in the admissions process," he said. "Most colleges will use the SAT as one piece of evidence, but a lot of them will use it to weed out a whole lot of kids who never then get a chance."[7]

In 2019, the standardized test score numbers were even worse for children in New York City in specialized schools than they were in the 1990s.

"Only seven out of 895 admits to Stuyvesant were black, as opposed to 587 Asian and 194 white students. Only 12 out of the 803 students admitted to the Bronx High School of Science were black, and only 95 out of 1,825 students admitted to Brooklyn Tech. This is all in a city in which 26 percent of public school students are Black."[8]

Ever since the Supreme Court's historic *Brown v. Board of Education* decision desegregated America's schools in 1954, black people have struggled to gain equal educational access and resources. Like so many other institutions, the American system of education, with its weak foundation, has set up black and brown people to fail. This is why President Lyndon Johnson once identified poverty as the "greatest barrier" to educational opportunity and provided $1 billion for schools with large numbers of poor children, under Title I.

It is commonly known that black students do not see any relevance in many of the subjects that they are taught. Personally, I relate to these youth. When I was a child, I told my mother after school on

---

7 Jessica Prois. "Does the SAT Have a Racial Bias?" *HuffPost*. Dec. 2017.
8 John McWhortor. "Don't Scrap the Test; Help Black Kids Ace It." *The Atlantic*. 9 May 2019.

different occasions that school was boring and much of what I was learning did not pertain to me. I felt unchallenged and unmotivated, especially in subjects like religion and history. Much of the global and American history that black children learn from the textbooks is truth mixed with falsehood. Historically, these textbooks have omitted black people and our contributions to civilized society.

Hence, the American educational system has been a conduit of white supremacy. Similar to the effect that termites have on wood, the lies our children digest deteriorates their self-esteem which, ultimately, kills their motivation. Like other children, black and brown youth need to see and hear about the accomplishments of their ancestors. The creations of black inventors and scientists is at best only highlighted during Black History month, and our children are given a consistent overdose of the sugarcoated narrative about Dr. Martin Luther King, Jr. As Cheryl Fields-Smith, a professor of education at the University of Georgia states, "If you only go to public schools, and that's the only place you're educated, then you learn that your history began with slavery, and it pretty much ended with MLK."

Our children are rarely taught about rebellious and militant freedom fighters such as Nat Turner, Huey P. Newton, Queen Nzingha, and Winnie Mandela. Why is that? It is done systematically because those leaders are not on the "approved" list, as it pertains to white supremacy. Nat, Huey, Queen Nzingha, and Winnie do not fit into the passive narrative that many in white America prefer young black boys and girls to follow. It is easy to point the finger at classroom teachers for neglecting to offer instruction about some of these heroes and sheroes. However, the racial bias and unwitting ignorance makes many administrators, curriculum specialists and content leaders all look guilty in my eyes.

Meanwhile, black/brown children are taught about America's Founding Fathers in glowing terms. They are told in a footnote, at best, that President George Washington, President Thomas Jefferson, and many others were slaveholders, who could not have believed that "all men are created equal," as stated in the Declaration of Independence. I state this because only eleven years after the Declaration of Independence was written, in 1787, black people were classified as three-fifths of a human being at the Constitutional Convention.

Moreover, our children are not educated about the whole truth regarding President Abraham Lincoln. Mr. Lincoln was more of a savvy politician than humanitarian, as our children are made to believe. President Lincoln's own words speak to this. He stated at the 1858 Presidential Debate in Charleston, Illinois: "I am not nor ever have been in favor of bringing about in any way the social and political equality of white and the black races."

Surely, this distortion or omission of facts in American elementary and high school textbooks is not an accident. These historical exclusions lead to a false sense of white superiority, as well as a mindset of black inferiority. Consequently, it is not an accident that some of our children are uninterested in going to school. It is also not by chance that some school systems couldn't care less about educating and empowering black and brown children.

New York City has one of the largest school districts in the nation. After surveying New York's Department of Education reading list, I found the DOE's list culturally uninteresting. After I observed the reading lists for sixth through eighth graders in particular, the *Narrative of the Life of Fredrick Douglass* and *To Kill a Mockingbird* were the only books with storylines that included black people. Most of the other books, such as *The Old Man and the Sea* and *My Side of the Mountain*, and many others have no cultural relevance to the lives of children from communities such as Brownsville, the South Bronx, and Lefrack City. This is even more so the case with Generation Z, which grew up gaining most of their information from social media like YouTube.

America admits that it lacks equality in its school system when it is forced to pass laws such as the No Child Left Behind. This policy grew out of the concern that the American education system was no longer competitive internationally. No Child Left Behind existed from 2002-2015. Its goal was to hold schools accountable for how children learned and achieved. That premise alone is alarming because it makes me question who was being held accountable before this act was put in place.

The Every Student Succeeds Act (ESSA) was signed by President Obama in 2015 to replace the No Child Left Behind law. The ESSA works to uphold the critical protections that are in place for students who come from disadvantaged families. Like No Child Left Behind, school accountability is centered on test scores which, as stated earlier, is an unreliable way of judging academic potential.

These laws and others that are enacted seem to miss the racial and socioeconomic factors that cause issues with the learning process. These new educational policies inevitably indict the last one that existed. For parents of black and brown children, it is a constant reminder that the system has failed them generation after generation.

"The public education system is undeniably flawed. Yet many of the deepest flaws have been deliberately cultivated. Funding inequity and racial segregation, for instance, aren't by-products of a system that is broken. They are direct consequences of an intentional concentration of privilege. Placing the blame solely on teacher training, or the curriculum, or on the design of the high school—alleging "brokenness"—perpetuates the fiction that all schools can be made great without addressing issues of race, class, and power."[9]

In the American school system, there is also low morale among teachers.

"Teachers, for instance, have seemingly never been more disillusioned. Roughly half of teachers report feeling under great stress

---

[9] Jack Schneider. "America's Not-So-Broken Education System." *The Atlantic*. 22 Jun 2016.

several days a week; job satisfaction is at a 25-year low, and almost a third of teachers say they are likely to leave the profession within the next five years. Parents, too, have never had less confidence in the system."

My fiancée, Najuma, is a teacher in the NYC public school system and consistently comes home stressed and exhausted, to say the least. According to the most recent Phi Delta Kappa/Gallup poll, "roughly 80 percent of Americans give grades of "C," "D," or "F" to the nation's schools—a far larger total than the 56 percent who issued those grades three decades ago."

Yes, the school system is bleeding, our children are hurting, and the teachers are burned out. Therefore, the false premise of the student-athlete starts way before they walk the halls of a high school or college. For example, when I coached, I dealt with many young men who came into my high school with reading levels that were below fifth grade. How did that happen? How were they allowed to advance to the next grade levels?

I am not naive enough to think that I can reform the Department of Education in this country; however, by nature, I am an optimist when it comes to black children. So many in our society see reincarnated versions of "Detroit Red" who was a pimp and street hustler before he cleaned up his life through the teachings of the Nation of Islam and became known to the world as Malcolm X. Like the Honorable Elijah Muhammad foresaw in Malcolm, I see redemptive qualities in these young men. I also see mini-Paul Robesons in these brothers. I believe our children have the ability to stand out academically and athletically, just as Mr. Robeson stood out at Rutgers University before going on to be one of the most prominent figures of the Harlem Renaissance. In our children, I see leaders, great fathers, eloquent lawyers, brilliant mechanics, selfless teachers, civilized corrections officers and, of course, talented athletes.

Unfortunately, many who work in the school system do not have the same perception of young black boys and girls. A lot of teachers who work with our children have low expectations for them. Dr. Jawanza Kunjufu states:

"The University of Chicago conducted a study of 70,000 schools trying to determine the major factor in student performance. The most important factor in student performance is not parent demography or how much money the school has, but teacher/parent expectations."

Too many teachers, regardless of race, are in the profession to pick up a check. There are plenty of so-called educators from outside of my community who lack an organic attachment and don't even strive to have one.

I have served as a teacher and counselor in the Department of Education and have witnessed the cultural disconnect many teachers have when dealing with black boys. Some white teachers lack patience when dealing with young black men and are often not equipped to deal with the source from where their issues derived. These teachers will quickly label the student a "problem child" who has Attention Deficit Hyperactivity Disorder (ADHD). Too often, a lot of our boys are assessed with this conduct disorder and other ailments. Dr. Umar Johnson, a school psychologist, emphatically urged parents to tell these teachers "to stop, your expertise is in teaching, it is not in mental diagnosis."

Dr. Donna Ford, a Professor of Education and Human Development at Vanderbilt, wrote in a *New York Times* op-ed:

"Boys tend to be more active than girls, and African-Americans are known for being movement-oriented, tactile and kinesthetic. This is considered normal and healthy in the African-American community, but, not necessarily so, in schools."[10]

---

[10] Donna Ford. "Don't Rush to Saddle Children with the A.D.H.D Label." *NYTimes.com*. 1 Feb 2016.

What does that look like in a classroom of eight-year-old boys where the diagnosis starts? Blurting out an answer, losing homework, not being able to pay attention, excessive energy. What eight-year-old do you know who is not HYPER?

The synonym in basketball for being hyperactive is having a "high motor." In fact, a high level of energy is a positive trait of many great NBA players such as Russel Westbrook, Dennis Rodman, and Kobe Bryant. Dr. Ford also stated,

"Of course, a small number of students from all cultural, racial, and gender groups do have A.D.H.D. needs. However, I am convinced that the pervasiveness of this label is a product of prejudice and discrimination--intentional by some, and unintentional by others. Either way, too many black males are inaccurately labeled as having A.D.H.D."[11]

What happens after being diagnosed with ADHD? Prescriptions for such medications as Adderall and Vyvanse follow. The side effects of Adderall can be mood swings, nervousness, faster heart rate, headaches, dizziness, insomnia. The side effects of Vyvanse can be insomnia and irritability. The side effects of both medicines can be just as bad, if not worse, than the original symptoms.

In my humble opinion, the best medicine for student athletes that I have coached who have been improperly labeled with ADHD is love, understanding, and respect. A simple arm around the shoulders, candid heart to heart conversations, home visits, and consistent dialogue with their family members go a long way. As someone who has coached, mentored, counseled, and given tough, as well as emphatic, love to my players, I believe in a more holistic approach to teaching. I don't think our children need more medicine; I believe they need more unconditional love and attention. It is estimated that 85% of black boys without fathers are labeled with ADHD, prompting Dr.

---

[11] Donna Ford. "Racism and Sexism in Diagnosis A.D.H.D." NYTimes.com. 13 Oct. 13.

Umar Johnson to give ADHD a new meaning, "AINT NO DADDY AT HOME SYNDROME." I concur emphatically with this acronym.

Teachers who sacrifice their time and effort to acquaint themselves with a culture that is not their own ultimately show respect to t heir students. Unfortunately, there is often minimal relationship building by teachers who are not familiar with black and brown cultures.

Lack of empathy often serves as an immediate excuse to place young black boys in special education.

"Black boys often arrive in kindergarten classrooms with inherent disadvantages; they continue to experience a "behind the 8-ball" mentality as their school careers progress. Black boys are more likely than any other group to be placed in special education classes with 80 percent of all special education students being black or Hispanic males."[12]

As a mentor/coach, I have worked with so many young men who have been labeled as Special Ed. What I have witnessed more than anything is that when they have a sense of structure and discipline, like any other young man, they can thrive. It is also known that black and brown children receive zero tolerance and often are placed in handcuffs when they misbehave. According to the Department of Education statistics, 70 percent of students arrested at school during the 2009-2010 school year were black and Latino.

Moreover, what is often overlooked or ignored is the role that elements of poverty, including air or lead pollution, play in increased levels of children being placed in Special Ed.

"Since African American, Hispanic, and low-income families are more likely to live in close proximity to sources of pollution like toxic waste and toxics release inventory, where housing is less expensive,

---

[12] Matthew Lynch. "4 Troubling Truths about Black Boys and the US Educational System." Aug. 2105.

it is possible that exposure to pollution is one mechanism through which poverty produces negative cognitive and health outcome."[13]

For example, "three years after the crisis began, the percentage of third graders in Flint who passed Michigan's standardized literacy test dropped from 41% to 10%." Dr. Mona Hanna-Attisha, the courageous warrior who dropped the first bomb in the Flint crisis by linking the water in Flint to high levels of lead in the area's children stated, "There is no safe level of lead... It is an irreversible neurotoxin. It attacks the core of what it means to be you, and impacts cognition--how children think," Hanna- Attisha says. "[Lead] actually drops IQ levels. It impacts behavior, leading to things like developmental delays."

She has estimated that "14,000 Flint children under the age of six were exposed."[14] It has recently been widely reported that Jackson, Mississippi, a city that is comprised of a majority of black people is also facing an emergency water shortage.

What are the solutions? While picking up and moving from a toxic environment to a less polluted community with a better education system sounds like a good plan, it is not realistic for many families who are financially strapped. However, with an awakened consciousness, these families are not hopeless. I believe our solution begins with truth. As Jesus said in John verse 8:32, "And the truth shall set you free."

In their child's early development years, I think black parents need to seek out schools that are deeply based in black culture. As our children learn of their rich culture, it will help them develop a strong sense of self awareness, self-esteem, self-determination, and self-respect. A strong sense of self will help the black child navigate

---

[13] Claudia Persico. "How exposure to pollution affects educational outcomes and inequality." *Brookings*. 20 Nov 2019.
[14] 60 *Minutes*. "Overtime Long lines for Water and New Evidence of Long-Term Health Impact on the Children of Flint." 12 Mar 2020.

with confidence through a society that often attacks their psyche both subtly and openly.

If possible, we need to seek out schools that have black male teachers for boys and black female teachers for our young sisters. It has been my experience that black youth need to see and be taught by educated, professional, older reflections of themselves. I have found that many young brothers have a need to be educated by black men who are capable of code switching with relatable swag and slang. I would also suggest adding homeschooling as an option to educate your child for a few years, if possible, and adding healthy doses of black history.

Professional athletes who have been homeschooled in the past include Justin Jackson, who attended the University of North Carolina before being drafted by the Dallas Mavericks. Justin attended Homeschool Christian Youth Association (HCYA), a non-profit Christian service organization created to serve homeschool families in Houston and the surrounding area. Six -time NBA all-star Blake Griffin, now playing for the Brooklyn Nets, was homeschooled until attending high school at Oklahoma Christian School. (As an aside, my Bishop Loughlin team beat Griffin's high school team by over 20 points in the Slam Dunk to the Beach tournament in 2007.) Tennis stars Venus and Serena Williams were also homeschooled in elementary and middle school.

According to The National Home Research Institute (NHERI), the numbers of black parents choosing to homeschool their children has doubled in a little over a decade. About 220,000 black school-aged children are being homeschooled, up from estimates of 103,000 in 2003.

Traditionally, white homeschooling families cite religious or moral disagreements with public schools in their decision to homeschool. Studies indicate black families are more likely to cite the culture of low expectations for black students, or dissatisfaction with how their children—especially boys—are treated in schools.

In her own studies, Cheryl Fields-Smith, an Associate Professor in the Department of Educational Theory and Practice at the University of Georgia, has found similar motivations among black homeschoolers. She says bluntly,

"The schools want little black boys to behave like little white girls, and that's just never going to happen. They are different.... I think black families who are in a position to homeschool can use homeschooling to avoid the issues of their children being labeled 'trouble makers' and the suggestion that their children need special-education services because they learn and behave differently."

Black parents also cite "religious beliefs, a desire to shelter children from an increasingly crass or materialistic society, as well as racial bullying," as reasons for moving on from the traditional means of education. Additional studies show that black students are less likely to be recommended for gifted and advanced classes.

During Donald Trump's presidency, the rate of racial bullying in schools increased. Reports of teasing or put-downs because of race or ethnicity were nine percent higher in communities that supported Trump. Roughly 37 percent of students in Republican districts reported being bullied in 2017, compared with 34 percent in Democratic districts.[15]

No child should have to learn under these oppressive conditions. It is said that the definition of insanity is doing the same thing over and over while expecting different results. How can we continue to keep participating in a broken educational system and expect it to leave our children healthy and whole? At this point, thinking outside of the box is a necessity, as it pertains to educating our babies. Our children should no longer be taught by people who do not have high expectations for them and who, more importantly, do not provide the love and respect they deserve. As Brother Malcolm X once

---

[15] Kathiann Kowalski. "School bullying has risen in areas that Support Trump." *Science News for Students*. 30 Jan 2019.

stated, "Only a fool would let his enemy teach his children!" We can't afford to be unwise anymore.

KNOW THYSELF... THE AWAKENING OF THE BLACK ATHLETE

Know Thyself: Two powerful words that were first written on the temples in Kemit, or Egypt as the country is called today. The principle is a reference to possessing knowledge, wisdom, and understanding of self from a spiritual, historical, nutritional, and educational standpoint. It is very important that we empower young black athletes to know who they are beyond their physical prowess. They are, first, black boys or girls hailing from ancestors who are the fathers and mothers of civilization. It is a parent's duty to teach children about their rich history from the cradle. It is also the duty of coaches to teach players more than just basketball fundamentals and plays.

Our beautiful children need to understand early that they come from a lineage of some of the most powerful, brilliant, spiritual, moral, and ethical people who have ever existed. We come from great men, such as Mansa Musa of the Mali Empire, who is widely described as the wealthiest man ever to walk the earth. We are the descendants of Imhotep, a physician, architect, astrologer, and one of the first pyramid builders. We have 'in our blood,' the warrior King Menelek II who successfully fought off the Italians who were looking to conquer and colonize Ethiopia. We are the lineage of Yaa Asantewaa, Queen mother of Ejisu in the Ashanti Empire, who led the Ashanti war against British colonialists. They are only a few of the heroes and sheroes in our ancestry.

In the sports world, it is important that our young athletes understand that their ancestors paved the way. If it were not for their sacrifices, vision, and courage, we would not be here today as coaches or as players. In 1904, the game of basketball was first introduced to the black community in physical education classes in all-black schools in Washington, DC. Soon after, the era of the Black Fives would emerge. The Black Fives referred to all-black teams that played games in cities, mostly on the east coast. Traditionally, our people have always found the strength and vision to make something out of nothing, despite the odds. The same would hold true with our black basketball teams that thrived in the US between 1904 and 1950, when the NBA would not allow black athletes to play. They played in cities such as Chicago, New York, Washington, Philadelphia, Pittsburgh, and Cleveland, sometimes against other teams from other ethnic communities.

As a people, we stand on the shoulders of Robert Douglas who was nicknamed "Father of Black Professional Basketball" and who was the founder of the New York Renaissance (The Rens). He and the Rens barnstormed from the East to the Midwest. While going from city to city to play games, they often had to sleep and eat on the bus, since they were barred from many restaurants and hotels because of Jim Crow policies. At one point the Rens won 88 straight games against both black and white teams.

All of us owe much gratitude also to The Savoy Big Five, a semi-professional team founded in Chicago. Later, they changed their name to the Harlem Globetrotters in order to form an alliance with the mystique of the Harlem Renaissance, which was the black cultural revolution between 1918-1930 in Harlem, New York, and beyond.

We are indebted to Andrew "Rube" Foster, known as the "Father of Negro Baseball," and the architect of the Negro League in which my own great-grandfather, Ned Tarver Sr. ('Pop-Pop'), played. Foster was said to be inspired by the 1919 race riots in Chicago to form the Negro National League in 1920. Such greats as Jackie Robinson, Willie Mays, and Hank Aaron got their professional baseball start in the Negro Leagues.

The thread of our people defining their dignity in sports contin-ued with the likes of John Carlos and Tommie Smith, who won gold and silver medals, respectively, at the Olympics in New Mexico City in 1968. They stood up on the podium and thrusted their fists in the air with black gloves to protest the inequalities that black people faced in America. That imagery became an iconic photo reflective of the Black Power movement.

Other than my parents, my favorite person growing up was the heavyweight boxing champion Muhammad Ali. As a little boy, I found it to be an honor that he was born on January 17th, which was only one day after my birthday. I loved his confidence. On the wall in my bedroom, near my bunkbed, was a picture of him and his famous quote, "Float like a butterfly and sting like a bee."

Though I came to understand who he was at the end of his box-ing career, it was his bravado and bold black manhood that I found so appealing. He was a black alpha male, and he made no apologies about his beliefs and love for his people. He was non-submissive and non-negotiating when it involved the justices and rights of black and brown people. I was attracted to his spirit. He roared like the king of the jungle, and I was one of the many cubs he never met but still found a way to 'raise.'

Muhammad Ali once stated, "I know I got it made while the masses of black people are catchin' hell, but as long as they ain't free, I ain't free." As has been well recorded in history, Ali sacrificed his heavyweight title because he refused to be drafted into the Vietnam War. He said,

"Why should they ask me to put on a uniform and go 10,000 miles from home and drop bombs and bullets on brown people in Vietnam while so-called Negro people in Louisville are treated like dogs and denied simple human rights? No, I'm not going 10,000 miles from home to help murder and burn another poor nation simply to con-tinue the domination of white slave masters of the darker people the world over. This is the day when such evils must come to an end. I have been warned that to take such a stand would cost me millions of dollars. But I have said it once and I will say it again. The real enemy of my people is here."

What a man!

Decades later, other voices would rise out of America's most precious institutions such as the NFL, like former San Francisco 49er quarterback Colin Kaepernick. In 2017, Kaepernick peacefully took a knee during the play of the National Anthem to protest police brutality and racial injustice in America. His detractors carefully attempted to remix the reason for his protest, diminishing it and re-casting it as a disrespectful act against the American flag. Former New Orleans quarterback Drew Brees supported the same fabricated narrative, stating in an interview:

"I will never agree with anybody disrespecting the flag of the United States of America or our country, I love and respect my teammates, and I stand right there with them in regard to fighting for racial equality and justice. I also stand with my grandfathers who risked their lives for this country, and countless other military men and women who do it on a daily basis."

Richard Sherman, the current cornerback of the Tampa Bay Buccaneers, "clapped back" at Drew stating,

"I guarantee you there were black men fighting alongside your grandfather, but this doesn't seem to be about that. That uncomfortable conversation you are trying to avoid by injecting military into a conversation about brutality and equality is part of the problem."

Days later, Brees acknowledged that his comments were "insensitive and completely missed the mark on the issues we are facing right now as a country...they lacked awareness and any type of compassion or empathy."[16]

---

[16] *Drew Reports News*. 4 Jun 2020.

From the onset of his protests, Colin stated why he would not stand for the national anthem:

"I am not going to stand up to show pride in a flag for a country that oppresses black people and people of color.... To me, this is bigger than football and it would be selfish on my part to look the other way. There are bodies in the street and people getting paid leave and getting away with murder."

He said this in 2016, before most of us ever knew the names of Jacob Blake, George Floyd, Breonna Taylor, Carlos Carson, Elijah McClain and so many other victims of racism and police brutality. Even in the midst of so much racial unrest in the country, former President Donald Trump stated, "For people to disrespect that by kneeling during the playing of our national anthem, I think it's disgraceful." Even the late Supreme Court Justice Ruth Ginsburg called the protest "dumb and disrespectful" when she spoke to journalist Katie Couric.[17]

I wondered, often, if Trump and many who shared his sentiment knew or even cared about the third stanza of the national anthem written by Francis Scott Key in 1814:

> No refuge could save the hireling and slave
> From the terror of flight or the gloom of the grave, And
> the star-spangled banner in triumph doth wave O'er the
> land of the free and the home of the brave.

By the time Key wrote these words, the British military included a regiment of former slaves called the Colonial Marines, whom the British encouraged to escape, and then trained and armed.[18]

Is not standing for the anthem still dishonorable? Would Mr. Trump and others ever find it disgraceful for Jews not to stand in

---

[17] *The Katie Couric Interview*. Yahoo Sports. 4 Nov 2016.
[18] Jefferson Morley, Jon Schwarz. "More Proof the U.S. National Anthem Has Always Been Tainted with Racism." *The Intercept*. 13 Sep 2016.

Germany for their flag and anthem, if they were still being oppressed by the hellish residue that Hitler left in the country?

It is important to know history. I could relate instantly to Colin's lack of reverence for the national anthem. Many years before, my mother emphatically told me to remain seated when the anthem played before NBA and MLB games that we attended. I can still remember a white man yelling at us to stand up. As his face turned red, his eyes were met with my mother's cold stare that was filled with memories of her ancestors' suffering and the lack of justice afforded to them. Perhaps Colin and my mother were inspired by Jackie Robinson, who stated once, "I cannot stand and sing the anthem. I cannot salute the flag; I know that I am a black man in a white world."

In 2014, LeBron James, Kyrie Irving, and other NBA players put on "I CAN'T BREATHE" shirts in response to viewing the video of Eric Garner being killed by the chokehold of Daniel Pantaleo of the NYC police department. Three years later, LeBron called Donald Trump "a bum" on Twitter in reaction to Trump disinviting Steph Curry to the White House after the Golden State Warriors won the NBA Championship. Over 1.5 million people liked LeBron's tweet, and as of December 5, 2020 it was retweeted 660,638 times.

Even Michael Jordan, who has been criticized in the past for being apolitical, recently took a stance on racial injustice. He donated $100 million from his Jordan Brand to organizations dedicated to promoting racial equality. "We have had enough," Jordan said in response to the George Floyd video. I write this chapter because our athletes cannot afford to play it safe anymore as long as our people are facing violence and oppression in all U.S. industries.

During the uprisings of 2020, the killings of George Floyd, Ahmaud Arbery, and Breonna Taylor were just the latest casualties of the torturing and killing of black people by police departments, which is an American tradition. The frustrations from this treatment have spilled into the streets all over America and around the world. People of all races have hit the streets with signs saying, DEFUND THE POLICE,

WHITE SILENCE IS COMPLIANCE, FUCK THE POLICE BLACK LIVES MATTER and more. These protests are teaching moments for all of us to learn about who and why and what is going on in this country.

Parents, teachers, and coaches have a responsibility to teach our babies the truth of what they are up against. Our children need to be raised consciously so that when they are in position, they can pay the blessings forward. We need more Craig Hodges, Mahmoud Abdul-Raufs, Jim Browns and others who have looked fear in the eyes, and, even when trembling, used their platforms to effect change for their people.

Some of our WNBA sisters have stood tall in their quests to make change. Maya Moore, who won two gold medals at the Olympics, four WNBA championships, a WNBA finals MVP in 2013, and a WNBA MVP in 2014, sacrificed two WNBA seasons as she advocated publicly for the release of a black man named Jonathan Irons, whom she eventually married. Mr. Irons was wrongly convicted in 1998 for burglary and assault. Maya helped pay for his defense team and worked religiously to free him from prison. He was released on July 1, 2020, from Jefferson City Correctional Center (Missouri). Maya Moore is now one of the undisputed heavyweight champions for social justice; she has walked the same journey as heroes like Muhammad Ali and John Carlos.

As much as we are raising great athletes, it is more important that we teach them early how to use their platforms for substance. I was proud to see the young tennis phenom Cori 'Coco' Gauff, who posted a moving video on her social media in tribute to George Floyd and others. She had 679,000 viewers on Instagram. She stated, "If you are choosing silence, you are choosing the side of the oppressor."

We are living in a beautiful era, where college athletes are increasingly using their social media platforms to advance racial progress as well. Kylin Hill, the star running back for the University of Mississippi, stated that he would not represent the state until the Mississippi flag is changed. The Mississippi State flag had the Confederate flag within it and Mississippi was the only state flag within the union that bore the Confederate design. He said in a tweet, "Either change the flag or I won't be representing this State anymore & I meant that. I'm tired." The Governor of Mississippi, Tate Reeves, recently signed a law to change the flag after the state legislature passed the bill.

> And everybody knows about Mississippi goddam This is a
> show tune
> But the show hasn't been written for it, yet Hound dogs on
> my trail
> School children sitting in jail Black cat crosses my path
> I think every day's going to be my last Lord have mercy on
> this land of mine We all gonna get it in due time
> I don't belong here
> —Nina Simone (Mississippi Goddamn)

WHEN THE AIR COMES OUT OF THE BALLS

Currently, there are only two owners of color in the NFL: Jacksonville Jaguars owner, Shahid Khan, who is Pakistani American, and Kim Pegula, who is Asian American, and who co-owns the Buffalo Bills. No black person has ever owned an NFL franchise. Major league baseball only has one principal owner who is a person of color, Arte Moreno, a Mexican-American. In the NBA, Michael Jordan is the principal owner of the Charlotte Hornets; Sacramento Kings owner, Vivek Ranadivé, is Indian-American; and Milwaukee Bucks co-owner, Marc Lasry, is Moroccan-American. At the time of this writing the NBA recently launched an investigation to look into claims from dozens of current and former employees that Robert Sarver, the owner of the Phoenix Suns, has a long history of racist and misogynistic incidents. So, perhaps, the face of that ownership will change soon.

According to SBnation.com, of the 77 rookie NBA head coaches hired over the past twenty years, "thirty-one of them never played in the NBA. Only five of those, or 16 percent, are coaches of color. This, in a league in which more than 80% of the players are men of color." They go on to say, "Over the past five years, white men have gotten 38 percent of the jobs given to rookie head coaches with NBA playing experience despite being seventeen percent of the player pool. Over the past twenty years, 46 former players have been hired as first-time head coaches, 65 percent of them are men of color, despite 83 percent of NBA players being men of color."

In the year 2021, seven out of the 30 NBA coaches were black. In the 2021 NBA Eastern and Western conference finals, three out of the four head coaches were black. This shows and proves that we are more than capable to lead franchises, we just need the opportunities. The NBA has shown progress on this matter in the 2021 off-season, as seven out of the eight head coaching vacancies were filled by black men.

During the time I worked for the New Jersey Nets, before they moved to Brooklyn, I worked for four general managers. Out of the four, three were white. Currently, there are ten black general managers in the NBA: Koby Altman of the Cleveland Cavaliers; Marc Eversley of the Chicago Bulls; Scott Perry of the New York Knicks; Brian Wright of the San Antonio Spurs; Troy Weaver of the Detroit Pistons; Calvin Booth of the Denver Nuggets; Nico Harrison of the Dallas Mavericks; James Jones of the Phoenix Suns; Trajan Langdon of the New Orleans Jazz; and Elton Brand of the Philadelphia 76ers. James Jones was named the 2021 NBA Executive of the Year. As stated earlier, the majority of NBA players are black and there are 30 teams in the league. Can you imagine this type of discrepancy existing in other sports? According to a Mark Spears tweet, one anonymous Black Assistant GM stated, "If 75% of the NHL's GMs were black, I'm sure it would be a big issue."

As I write this, the NFL has only two black head coaches in a 32-team league where three-quarters of the players are black men. The representation among the 32 teams' top front-office executives is eleven percent. This despite the Rooney Rule, an NFL policy requiring teams to interview ethnic-minority candidates for head coaching and senior football operation jobs. Since the Rooney Rule was implemented in 2003, only fifteen black head coaches have been hired out of 129 candidates. These are some of the statistics that earned a failing grade from Richard Lapchick, the director of the Institute for Diversity and Ethics in Sport. Recently, the former coach of the Miami Dolphins, Brian Flores, filed a 58-page lawsuit against the NFL alleging discrimination in his head coaching interviews with the New York Giants and the Denver Broncos.

In Major League Baseball, there have been only five African American GMs in history, and three franchises still have never hired a minority to be their GM or manager: the St. Louis Cardinals, Minnesota Twins, and Oakland Athletics. Dusty Baker, now the current Houston Astros manager who has led five different franchises to a division title, and led the Los Angeles Dodgers to a World Championship, only received one job interview after leading the Washington Nationals to back-to-back division titles in 2016 and 2017. He stated,

"I don't know where it's going, but we've gone backwards in a lot of ways. I get guys calling me asking how to deal with the system, saying things aren't fair or equal. Well, it's a whole lot less than equal now. It's just getting worse."

While sports are the calling card for so many black and brown youth in urban communities, it is not realistic to think that most will ever play professionally. According to Livestrong.com, three out of 10,000 male high school basketball players will be drafted into the NBA, or about .03 percent. Yes! Those are low numbers, yet for so many people who have had the odds stacked against them from birth, becoming an athlete often seems like the only way out of the hood.

The dream is chased starting from early childhood years. Black boys often walk around with blinders on. In poverty-laced neighborhoods, there is limited hope, and even worse, restricted avenues to creating a better lane for oneself. Playing ball, rapping, drug dealing, pimping, stripping, scamming credit cards, and even gangbanging dominate the psyche in terms of what it will take to make a living. As the legendary rapper Biggie Smalls eloquently stated, "Either you are slinging crack rock, or you got a wicked jump shot."

In my years of scouting for the Nets, I had been asked on numerous occasions to speak at Career Days at many schools. I always chose to highlight the different careers in sports that children can pursue to earn a living. Most of the young brothers and sisters had no idea about the different opportunities that exist.

When I speak about the profession of scouting, the curiosity in the room is always enormous. Questions flow in rapid succession. "You mean, they pay you to go around the country and watch games?" "Do they feed you too?" "You mean, you can go to almost any NBA game in the country for free?"

Of course, my job entailed more than that; however, it is a blessing to share my experiences with these excited and impressionable children. I never underestimate how much it means to them to listen to someone who looks like them and still lives in their community. While working for the Nets, I felt it was my duty to take advantage of my platform in order to help my community.

Nothing brought that home more than November 2014. I was sitting in my living room and the video of a young black boy being shot was going viral on all social media platforms. The boy, Tamir Rice, was twelve years old when he was playing with a toy gun in the Cudell Recreation Center in Cleveland, Ohio. Policemen Timothy Loehmann and Frank Garmback were responding to a call that a male was randomly pointing a gun. On the call, they were told twice that the "pistol was probably fake." Loehmann, who was a rookie police officer at the time, shot Tamir less than two seconds after arriving on the scene. Later, it was revealed that Loehmann had been deemed emotionally unstable and unfit for duty, yet he had hidden that from the Cleveland police department. A grand jury declined to indict the policemen and the FBI ruled that Loehmann's "response was a reasonable one."

Tamir's death affected me personally. He was the same age as so many young brothers I once coached. His face looked bright and smooth; his smile was warm and oozing with hope. My emotions raced from depression, rage, and hopelessness to fatigue and anger. I knew that a little white boy in the same circumstances would not have been harmed. I was already prepared also for the police to get a slap on the wrist, at best, for the murder.

This was yet another message from the state that black bodies were expendable, and black males were the number one target. As I watched the marches and protests on television, I became even more frustrated. I was aware of the pacifying baby formula we would be given. The media would find the local preacher and politicians and give them the microphone to make sure black people stayed peaceful.

In the more than 50 years since the March on Washington, we are still protesting the same issues! More than 50 years since fourteen-year-old Emmett Till was brutally lynched and his body was muti-lated—and here we are again. I was—and still am—tired of marching and protesting. I have participated in my share of both over the years. Tamir's death would reawaken the proactive gene inside me. Tamir was one of the latest martyrs of the struggle.

The end of his life was a second birth for my Brooklyn Bridge Basketball program which, until then, had remained dormant in deference to my scouting duties. At that point, I felt my ancestors calling my name to get off the sidelines. Thus, I started my second Brooklyn Bridge journey with volunteer coaches and ten-year-old players. Our goal was to serve as The Bridge to college. I pledged to be The Bridge to professional sports for black youth, and I am still on that mission today.

I began to take advantage of the relationships I cultivated while working for the Nets in order to benefit the youth in my program.

I invited many people from various professions in the industry to share some of their time and knowledge with the youth in my organization. The first person I invited to speak to my players was the Nets' head athletic trainer, who did a free training for the children in a local park. He also answered questions regarding his job and how he started his career.

Rondae Hollis Jefferson, the Nets' 2015 first round draft pick, graciously took time out of his schedule to host a basketball camp for our program. Also, former Nets head coach, Kenny Atkinson, hosted a basketball clinic. He was completely hands-on and passionately participated in every drill.

The children and parents received so much from these experiences. However, the long-term effect was what I was most concerned about. I wanted children from my hood to see themselves in the same shoes as these professionals. I hoped these children would one day pay the blessing forward for the next generation.

Whenever I could, I would obtain tickets to games for my Brooklyn Bridge children and gave them the access they deserved. I also formed a relationship with the Nets' equipment guy, who gave me boxes upon boxes of sneakers, bags, socks, and shirts that the players did not want at the end of the season. I gladly took the free equipment and gave the gear to the children of my program.

As a man of the community, I had big ideas that I thought the Nets could implement. At one point, I wrote a proposal for the Brooklyn Nets Community Department. I wanted them to host seminars on careers in sports for youth in Brooklyn.

Because of the socio-economic disparities of black and brown children in the public school system, there are not that many entry-level programs that make high school students aware of the endless number of occupations in the sports industry. As a youth, I was not aware of the numerous career paths available in sports.

My good friend Fred Galloway, who is originally from Bedford-Stuyvesant, Brooklyn, is currently head of security for the Nets. He travels from city to city with the team and is responsible primarily for the well-being of the players. He is also the go-to-guy when it comes to keeping players from making bad decisions and is responsible for "putting out fires" surrounding the team. To my knowledge, every team, has a Head of Team Security, who has an extensive background usually in law enforcement. Prior to joining the Nets, Fred spent six years working as an investigator on an FBI counter terrorism team, after having worked in the New York Police Department's Intelligence Division.

I developed a relationship also with one of the Brooklyn Nets' team physicians, Riley J. Williams, III, who was also the team doctor for the USA basketball team at the 2021 Olympics. He is an orthopedic surgeon and specialist in knee, shoulder, and elbow surgery at Hospital for Special Surgery.

Like Fred, Riley is a black man who loves the game of basketball and developed a great career in the sports industry after excelling in another arena. There are so many other black and brown champions who work behind the scenes in the sports world. Attorneys work for the team also, as do chefs, sports psychologists, directors of information technology, and directors of public relations. However, we still need more!

Becoming a scout was a big deal for me. After a few years of experience, I yearned to do more in the basketball operations department. I wanted to expand my role within the organization, but I did not see many opportunities falling into my lap.

My visions for my life have always been broad. I challenged myself to go back to school and earned a master's degree in Sports Management from Columbia University. Attending school part-time for three years and scouting talent for the Nets was grueling and demanding. I also took classes online, on a few occasions participating during the halftimes of games I was scouting. On one occasion while going to school at Columbia, I had to take an online class at the baggage claim, right after landing from a seven-hour flight. Often, I had to finish papers at two and three in the morning, after having sent in scouting reports that were due the next day. I summoned every bit of discipline in my body to juggle the rigorous academics of Columbia University with the demands of being an NBA scout.

Ultimately, I never received a promotion while working for the Brooklyn Nets. However, I did add value to my personal portfolio in hopes of leveraging my experience and education, as I continue to prepare myself for future endeavors. As Whitney M. Young once stated, "It is better to be prepared for an opportunity and not have one than to have an opportunity and not be prepared."

One class stood out: my Basketball Analytics class. The class covered the mathematically based, data driven method of analyzing everything you could think of in basketball. I had an interest in the class because I was working for a general manager, Sean Marks, who is a big believer in analytics. Sean learned how to manage a team from the legendary RC Buford of the San Antonio Spurs, who is known to be a strong ally of the analytics movement. Sean demonstrated his respect for the field by creating an analytics department while remodeling the offices and adding elite technology.

I am no fool. If he respected analytics, I knew that I had to be more knowledgeable about what was being discussed. Hence, what I learned in class came in handy. I was happy to learn about such terms as effective field goal percentage, win shares, player efficiency rating, points per possession, and more.

Overall, some of the information was helpful, especially for the draft, where projecting players' future production and minimizing the risks of picking the wrong player is key. On the other hand, I found that some of the data was useless. Like many scouts I know who have either coached and/or played, part of the evaluation process is done based on our innate feel for a player's impact, toughness, and motor.

Any good scout has an eye for the unseen or the intangibles. For many of us, analytics often feels like overkill. I noticed that most of the people who worked in basketball analytics departments were white men. I have been in many conversations with my peers, both black and white, who would grumble that analytics was just a new inroad for the inclusion of Ivy Leaguers and the Wall Street crowd to have a career in the NBA. ESPN analyst Amin Elhassan, who studied engineering at Georgia Tech and is a former assistant director of basketball operations with the Phoenix Suns, concurs:

"Don't tell me there aren't any black people on Wall Street who are passionate about basketball. These people exist. Wall Streeters, people with qualitative analysis backgrounds. I know them. I went to school with them. I just don't believe that one ethnicity is more predisposed to this than another. You realize, of course, that this is the new gateway into the game, into sports?"[19]

The analytics world has also affected the way of life of head coaches. Most coaches are expected to have a vested interest in analytics and how the use of it can help them scheme defensively, offensively and, ultimately, lead them to victory. Working in the league, it was standard to see head coaches meeting or walking around with one of our analytics staff members. The analytics guy would often have a laptop in hand, as he went over game plan.

In 2016, ESPN's Stephen A. Smith raised the alarm when discussing how analytics was impacting the hiring of black head coaches in the NBA, in particular. He said,

---

[19] Michael Wilbon. "Mission Impossible African-Americans & analytics." *The Undefeated*. 24 May 2016.

"That's the language the owners love to hear...and at the rate it's going, don't be surprised if in a league where there are 30 teams, and obviously, 30 head coaches, if ten percent or less of them happen to be black. Black coaches, head coaches are becoming an endangered species. They are in a world of trouble."

When the Brooklyn Nets hired Steve Nash to become their head coach, many people in the industry found the choice a racially insensitive one. Many believed their black interim head coach, Jacque Vaughn, should have been hired, after having led the Nets to a 5-2 record in the 2020 COVID "bubble."

Nevertheless, the hall of famer Nash was hired even though he had never even been an assistant coach in the league. In his first NBA coaching job, Nash was awarded the chance to coach three future hall of famers in their prime: Kyrie Irving, James Harden, and Kevin Durant. This is the equivalent of a child getting a Bentley sedan from their parents as his/her first car. Stephen A. Smith called it out for what it was—white privilege—on the show First Take on September 3, 2020. Steve Nash even concurred during his first press conference as Nets' head coach, stating, "I did skip the line, frankly."

If analytics is the language that NBA front offices speak, it is the aspiring black coach's duty to become well versed in it. While it may be true that analytics is being used as a way to keep black and brown people from elevating in the industry, I have one question: What else is new? It is up to us to make the adjustments and find a way. In the words of Denver Nuggets assistant coach and my brother, Popeye Jones, "Real ones know how to eat soup with a fork."

Our children need to understand that to obtain positions of employment in the sports industry, it takes an enormous amount of discipline, education, perseverance, and NETWORKING skills. I highlighted the word networking because, as the saying goes, "It is not what you know, but who you know." At some point, we all have to ask ourselves, "What are you willing to do to get where you want to get?" What does that mean? In all industries of America, black people, in particular, are conditioned in professional settings to be what I call "extra-professional." As Maurice Joseph, former head coach of George Washington University stated,

"There is a distinct consciousness about remaining polished in a professional setting when you're black. It goes beyond dressing appropriately and conducting yourself professionally. It's changing your accent, tweaking your personality, fitting the standards. Almost like you need to put on a show or else you will be perceived poorly."

Often, when we earn positions of authority, we are still not granted the same amount of power because of our skin color. We are seen by our own and others as the "token negro" or the "honorary white person." We are expected to have an even-keel temperament in corporate America at all times. This is no different than what Jackie Robinson had to deal with as a player, even though he was constantly disrespected.

We may be well equipped to speak on racial issues that may inevitably come up on the job, but, inherently, we know it is best that we "put our heads in the sand" or look the other way. If we challenge something on the job that we feel is racially insensitive, we are accused of playing the "race card." We are also keenly aware that to be labeled as the "angry black man or woman" is not a wise career move. I knew very well that I had to pick and choose my spots when dealing with some of my peers in the NBA who had made statements that I found racially insensitive. Therefore, like a good fighter, I learned how to bob and weave in the corporate ring. I knew I had to jab when needed and pull out the uppercut only as a last resort. This is the reality for many black men and women in all industries in America, and it does not exclude the world of sports.

My mother used to tell me that, to succeed, as a black man I must "work twice as hard, be twice as smart, be twice as dependable, and be twice as talented." So many black and brown professionals have found out that despite all the blood, sweat and tears that we spill to make it, often we only break even, at best, with our white counterparts, who may have less experience and fewer credentials. Recent data from the National Bureau of Economic Research stated, "Black workers receive extra scrutiny from bosses, which can lead to worse performance reviews, lower wages, and even job loss." The NBER paper, authored by Costas Cavounidis and Kevin Lang of Boston University, "attempts to show how discrimination factors into company decisions and creates a feedback loop, resulting in racial gaps in the labor force."

After all, in the year 2020, why would the NFL have to make amendments to the previously written 2002 version of the Rooney rule, which was aimed at improving diversity in coach and front-office hiring? One of the new rules of the Rooney Rule "is expanded to apply to several executive positions. Teams and the league office are now required to interview "minorities and/or female applicants" for positions such as team president and "senior executives in communications, finance, human resources, legal, football operations, sales, marketing, sponsorship, information technology, and security positions."

Former Chicago Cubs President, Theo Epstein, who endorsed the Black Lives Matter Movement after seeing George Floyd killed on video, stated,

"The majority of people that I hire, if I'm being honest, have similar backgrounds to me and look a lot like me. And that's something that I need to ask myself, why? I need to question my own assumptions, my own attitudes. I need to find a way to do better. If we all take that approach in the industry—we need to. If there's one thing we've learned with systemic racism in general in this world, the system doesn't check itself. It's on each of us to take action and stand up and make some changes."[20]

---

[20] Mike Oz. "Cubs President endorses Black Lives Matter, says MLB's hiring practices need to change." *Yahoo Sports.* 8 Jun 2020.

I agree with Theo that the system doesn't check itself, which places added pressure on the few black and brown people who are in positions of authority to make a change and empower their own. It is no longer good enough to be the minority face that leads any company, if you do not have the chutzpah to employ and empower your own when qualified. Black and brown industry leaders of tomorrow must be ready to pay the blessings forward, as was likely done for them. They will need to be bold, smart, professional, savvy, proud, and powerful.

Historically, a lot of people from black and brown communities do not have the generational "hook-ups" that our white counterparts possess. In most instances, we don't come into a job as made-men or women. We do not benefit from the white privilege that is woven deeply in every industry in this country. However, we do have perseverance, intelligence, and determination like our ancestors displayed when facing some of the most challenging obstacles the world has ever seen. As Muhammad Ali once stated, "If my mind can conceive it, and my heart can believe it—then I can achieve it." To the parents and the youth who are reading this book, that quote emphatically applies to you!! Explore all the career paths that sports have to offer. Be extra-curious and go for it!!!!

CHAPTER 10

CHOOSING A COLLEGE COACH

During the college recruitment process, the assistant coach of an institution will do most of the initial recruiting. Ideally, he/she will be someone with a lot of personality and charm. That coach will do his/her best to gain the trust of your child and family.

NCAA rules and regulations govern the ways in which a college coach can recruit a high school player. The best recruiters develop strong relationships with players as early as possible. To get acquainted with potential prospects, the college coaching staff formally starts the process by sending questionnaire forms to athletes when they become sophomores in high school. Please note, these are wide-net forms that are sent out to many athletes in whom they might have even a minute level of interest. Athletes should not let the college logo on an envelope go to their head!

DETERMINING THE VALUE OF THE OFFER

Recently during the pandemic, there was a wave of eighth graders and freshmen in high school who received college "offers," while many college coaches had never seen the players compete. Players and parents should know that more times than none these offers are contrived by AAU and college coaches for their own agendas. While the player feels good that he/she received an early offer, it is done to keep the school in the mindset of the player, like a mental seed planted in fertile soil. Meanwhile, the college coach will always be looking for a player more talented. Also, the AAU coach gets to say,

"See, I got you an offer through my connections." A pure game of smoke and mirrors. Do not take the lack of recruitment personally. If you are not attracting the attention you are looking for, work harder.

The recruitment of athletes is a business game, and the players are the pawns on the chessboard. It is the coach's job to know the prospect's birthday, as well as their mother's favorite recipe. A good recruiter knows who the 'new bae' (partner) of the athlete is. It is their job to study the athlete and, often, they will tell the recruit what they want to hear. There is a big difference between the questionnaire form and the handwritten notes that are sent.

The handwritten notes are a clear indication that an athlete is truly being recruited. Similarly, the coach who comes to see the athlete play live is really recruiting them. Like a good NBA scout, the good recruiter studies body language, as well as a player's interactions with teammates and coaches. They want to know if you are really six-feet- eight or, actually, six-feet-five. They will evaluate how you face adversity on the court. Will you quit when your team is getting blown out or will you keep fighting?

While many coaches are honest, they are also in a very competitive business that comes with a lot of pressure. It is their job to deliver the target prospects for the head coach, which is one of the main reasons they were hired. My advice to parents and players is really simple: approach the process with minimal emotion. These coaches would not even know you existed if you were not playing sports, so the process should be a fair exchange. They want your services, and you might want what they have to offer in terms of a college scholarship.

Your child is the commodity in this process; student athletes should understand their value. Only five percent of college students will make it on to a college roster, and only two percent of college athletes make it onto a Division I roster. Also, with the new NCAA rules allowing college student athletes to put their name in the transfer portal after the season, the competition pool just got tougher. Most college coaches would rather put a seasoned college athlete from another program on their roster than an "unseasoned" high school player who is usually not ready to produce right away.

EVALUATING A POTENTIAL COACH

The main reason you pick a school should never be because of the relationship you have with the assistant coach. Why not? Because most assistant coaches want to be head coaches eventually. Therefore, even if they are recruiting you one year, they might not be at that school the following season. Assistant coaches are usually ambitious by nature. Once the head coach or the associate head coach displays their desire for you to come to their school, then it is to be taken seriously.

Be prepared to dig deep into the head coach's background in order to make an intelligent decision. I would research the coach's success at their previous schools. Try to talk to their former players and find out their opinion of their former coach. Are there any scandals from the coach's past that do not match with your core principles? Below are some questions for the head coach I would ask. Simultaneously, as you ask these questions, you should read the coach's body language.

- Why does he want you to come play for him/her?
- Does his system fit your playing style?
- What is the graduation rate at the school?
- Who else is he recruiting in your class?
- Where are you on the depth chart of the players the coach is recruiting at the same position?

- What position do they see you playing at the school? (It might not be the position you think)
- What is the three-year plan of the program?
- What are the immediate goals of the team?
- What are the chances that you will play in your first year?
- What is there to do in the town or on the campus?
- What activities away from the court are available to you child?
- What is the meal plan? What is the housing plan?
- How long does he have on his contract?

When taking an official visit, be proud of that moment. Your services are officially desired by the coaches; probably, you meet all the standards they are looking for in a student-athlete. I took an official visit to a university in the South with one of my players and his mother. We traveled by plane, and we all stayed in a hotel where each of us had a Jacuzzi in our rooms. We ate good food, and the coaching staff even took the player and me to a strip club, where the head coach had his own personal spot in the back for lap dances.

Needless to say, we had a ball; they certainly got our attention. The most annoying part of the trip, much like other official visits I have been on, was the relentless pursuit of the assistant coaches to try to get the player to sign the letter of intent on the spot. It is similar to going to a timeshare pitch where they wine and dine you before pressuring you to buy a property.

MAKING A CASE FOR HIRING BLACK COACHES

When choosing a coach, especially as it pertains to black players, I stress, unapologetically, a strong consideration for playing for black head coaches. As of 2019, black coaches were thoroughly underrepresented in the Big 5 conferences, which, predominantly, are comprised of black players.

According to the NCAA Demographics Database, in 2018, The Atlantic Coast Conference had three black head coaches; the Big 12 had two. The Big Ten has one black coach, with Juwan Howard at the helm now, and the Pac 12 does not have one black head coach. Conversely, black men account for 56 percent of the assistant coaches and black athletes accounted for 55 percent of the players in men's Division I college basketball Power 5 conferences, plus the Big East.

Recruiting is the bloodline of any college athletic program. White head coaches consistently benefit from the elite black players in college basketball which, of course, has lasting effects on a coach's generational wealth and personal legacy. I am not blaming these coaches for taking advantage of the opportunity; however, I do blame a system that caters to hiring white men as coaches.

Many coaches I have spoken with have told me there is something wrong with the way universities use search firms to hire coaches. "White presidents hire white search firms to hire white ADs, who hire those same white search firms to hire white head coaches."[21] Excluding HBCUs, currently only ten percent of Division I athletic directors are black.

Obviously, this formula gives white coaches an unfair advantage to lead programs, at the expense of their black counterparts. Why shouldn't black coaches benefit from coaching young men who look like them and come from the same culture and communities?

As Jamal Murphy wrote in 2019 for The Undefeated, "Black assistant coaches must be given opportunities to be more than recruiters and valued for more than simply knowing how to relate to the black players who dominate the game." Or, as J. A. Adande stated in 2017:

---

[21] Rob Dauster. "'It's very disappointing': The number of black head coaches continues to fall at college hoops' highest level." NBC Sports. 2 Mar 2020.

"[Black assistant coaches] take the jobs they can get and rise until they hit the glass ceiling, which often means an assistant coach with heavy recruiting responsibilities."[22]

To go further, a black assistant's first opportunity as a head coach usually is not enticing. Many times, the school is in a conference where the team has been a habitual loser and lacks resources. Hence, most black coaches are forced to take head coaching jobs that put them in a position to fail.

I am sure Coach Mike Krzyzewski, as great a leader as he is, would give a lot of credit for his whopping five NCAA championships and twelve Final Four appearances to the talent he has accumulated throughout his coaching career. That success has propelled Coach K to the Naismith Hall of Fame. He has coached some of the best players in the world. In 2018, Coach Krzyzewski's Duke salary was $9,000,000. In the 2018-2019 season, Coach Krzyzewski coached mega-star Zion Williamson, the number one pick in the 2019 NBA Draft. Sales traffic to the Duke basketball ticket page on Vivid Seats rose 82 percent in the 2018-2019 season.

Coach Krzyzewski's incredible legacy has allowed him to create an impressive coaching tree, enabling his assistant coaches and former players to get head coaching jobs. This list includes Mike Brey (Notre Dame), Tommy Amaker (Harvard), Quin Snyder (Utah Jazz), Johnny Dawkins (UCF), Bob Hurley (Arizona State), and Jeff Capel (University of Pittsburgh). This list does not include the countless assistant coaches, and even some GMs and assistant GMs in the NBA, including Trajan Langdon, with whom I worked at the Brooklyn Nets. Langdon is now the general manager of the New Orleans Pelicans. This is what power looks like in an industry.

As mentioned earlier, currently the Pac 12 has no black head coaches. Arizona's former head coach, Sean Miller, was the highest

---

[22] J. A. Adande. "Black assistant coaches get hurt the most in recruiting scandals." *The Undefeated.* 6 Oct 2017

paid coach in the Pac 12. Miller had an enormous amount of success in that conference, yet he never made it to the NCAA Final Four. He was the sixth highest-paid coach in all of college basketball, with a salary of $4,054,853 in 2018. For years, he benefited from the recruitment of players such as Rondae Hollis Jefferson, Lauri Markkanen, and Stanley Johnson.

Most of these eventual NBA players, including the number one pick in the NBA 2018 Draft, Deandre Ayton, were recruited by my friend Emanuel "Book" Richardson who is the current director for the Gauchos grassroots basketball program in New York City. In 2019, "Book" pleaded guilty for receiving money to pay players for their services with the Arizona basketball program. He was caught up in a federal sting that included assistant coaches from various universities such as USC, Auburn, and Oklahoma State. Book was sentenced to three months in prison and two months of supervised probation.

It cannot be overlooked that the first school to face sanctions in this ordeal was Oklahoma State. OSU's head coach is Mike Boynton, a black man from Brooklyn who played high school ball at Bishop Loughlin. Before the 2020 season he was the lowest paid head coach in the Big 12 conference. The university was recently banned from the postseason in the spring of 2021 because one of the assistant coaches of the program used money to steer athletes to financial advisers. At all these institutions, the assistant coaches who were punished (jail time for some) were black and were recruiting for white head coaches who claimed to have no knowledge of the "illegal" recruiting. Yeah, okay.

This prompted college basketball analyst Len Elmore to say in the Jamal Murphy article in *The Undefeated*: "In the end, if you can bring in a great player without any corruption attached to it, [head coaches] will be happy. They don't want to know about it. It's hear no evil, see no evil."

These brothers were simply doing the grunt work that is required in recruiting for the benefit of the head coach and, ultimately, the university. Symbolically, it feels like an episode in *The Wire*, when street level drug dealers get caught up in a sweep, while the kingpins walk. Only this time, the characters of Stringer Bell and Avon Barksdale could be played by the likes of head coaches Sean Miller (formerly of Arizona) and Will Wade (formerly of LSU). Both coaches implicated themselves on a wiretap but were not indicted.

Ultimately, parents, players, AAU coaches, high school coaches, and mentors are on the front line with our youth and can play a tremendous role in influencing some of the elite players from our community to play for black coaches. Inevitably, there will be times at a school where your son or daughter plays when they will need to talk to someone that they can relate to culturally. Your son or daughter will need to lean on someone when racism rears its ugly head in the town or on the campus. As we have come to find out, the issues of society can be fluid.

The national uprisings that occurred after the killings of Breonna Taylor, George Floyd, Aubrey Taylor, and Rayshard Brooks have proved to be impactful. Your child will need to be with empathizing supporters. It would be intelligent to ask coaches who are recruiting your children where they stand on certain issues. For example, were they vocal or were they silent during the uprisings that occurred after George Floyd was murdered? Coach LeVelle Moton of North Carolina Central spoke boldly to this issue in the middle of the uprising.

"The reality is a lot of these coaches have been able to create generational wealth. Their grandkids' kids are gonna be able to live a prosperous life because athletes who were the complexion of George Floyd were able to run a football, throw a football, shoot a basketball or whatever have you to their benefit. But whenever people [who are] the complexion of George Floyd are killed, assassinated, murdered in the street in broad daylight, they're silent."

I was proud when Brooklyn Bridge Basketball alumnus Kyle Neptune, who was named recently as the head coach of Villanova University, called me for advice regarding the racial unrest that swept the U.S. in 2020 when he was a Villanova assistant. He felt compelled to do something with his platform. He did not feel he had been doing enough in past years to contribute towards making racial progress and he felt now was the time!

He rallied his peers who, at that time, were also top assistants at their respective universities, including Kimani Young, associate head coach at UConn, and Dwayne Killings, newly appointed head coach at the University of Albany. They formed a group called CFA—Coaches for Action. As Kyle stated after seeing the death of George Floyd on video, "I think all of us, everyone in the country, was moved by the recent events. We were moved to do something, not just be the type of people who say something needs to be done and not be doing anything."

Coach Killings stated, "We felt like it was our vision and our passion," noting that "we're all operating in the shadow of John Thompson," as a Big East coach who put his words into action.

They will be pushing their players to get active in the voting process. In 2020, they also pushed for their players to wear Black Lives Matter patches in support of the movement. I expressed to Kyle that I thought they should go further and push for a rule that mandates more opportunities for black coaches.

Recently, I joined Advancement of Blacks in Sports (ABIS), founded by my mentor, Gary Charles. On the ABIS website, it states that "Our mission is to connect and inspire people to boldly advocate for racial, social, and economic justice for blacks in sports." ABIS involves leaders in the sports industry, such as Florida State men's basketball head coach, Leonard Hamilton, University of South Carolina women's head coach Dawn Staley, and Hall of Fame Rutgers University former head coach Vivian Stringer. There are many more who are continuing to make strides towards significant changes in the sports industry.

Clemson head football coach, Dabo Swinney, two-time national champion, whose current salary is $9.3 million, came under fire for being tone deaf, at best, when putting on a "Football Matters" shirt in the middle of the 2020 racial uprisings. Many, including myself, felt that to wear this shirt in the middle of the BLACK LIVES MATTER movement was insensitive and disrespectful, to say the least. This callous disregard is from a man whose team consists mainly of black players and whose institution only integrated 57 years ago.

The Football Matters shirt worn by Dabo was compared to the All Lives Matter slogan that has been used by some people to take away the emphasis on "Black." This prompted Skip Bayless of Fox Sports 1 to tweet, "How is Dabo getting away with wearing that t-shirt, 'Football Matters', at this time? It's a slap in the face of every black man and woman in this country. You know it and I know it."

Swinney has also been called out by his former player, tight end D.J. Greenlee, who brought up a separate incident. DJ stated Clemson's assistant coach, Danny Pearman, used the N-word on numerous occasions during one of their practices. Greenlee tweeted, "You allowed a coach to call a player the N-word during practice with no repercussions . . . I will never understand why it was never addressed."

Coach Pearman has since apologized: "I know there is no excuse for me using the language in any circumstance. I never should have repeated the phrase. It was wrong when I said it, and it is wrong today. I apologized to D.J. at the conclusion of practice, who then appropriately raised his concern to Coach Swinney. Coach and I met to discuss the incident, and he reiterated that my language was unacceptable."[23] Pearman is currently the assistant head coach, tight ends coach, and special team's coordinator for the Tigers.

The current racial climate in America has brought about the exposure of coaches from other sports as well, such as former St. John's University fencing coach Boris Vaksman, who was recorded during

---

[23] "Clemson player DJ Greenlee recalls N word incident with coach." *The State*. 3 Jun 2020.

a private lesson saying black people "steal" and "kill," adding that he believed Abraham Lincoln "made a mistake." He went on to say, in an edited video, that Black people are troublemakers "because they don't want to work."[24] I wondered how the black students on the St. John's roster were treated, or mistreated, under the leadership of someone with this racist mindset.

Not too long ago, former Georgia Senator and the WNBA's Atlanta Dream co-owner Kelly Loeffler tweeted:

"Sports have the power to unite us, but @WNBA has embraced BLM—a radical movement that seeks to destroy American principles. I stand with @realDonaldTrump. I stand with the American flag, which has endured for 244 years. And I will not apologize for it."

Some of the sisters who play in the WNBA spoke up quickly regarding her statement, including Renee Montgomery, who played for the Dream and now is a part-owner. She stated, "Your comments hurt deeply because it was a veiled 'All Lives Matter' response," Montgomery wrote. "It's not that you're tone deaf to the cry for justice, but you seemingly oppose it. And you are speaking from a position of immense influence as a team co-owner in our league and as a U.S. Senator." I wonder what American principles Mrs. Loeffler was referring to?

As a scout, I have had my own issues during visits to college campuses. On some, in both the North and the South, I could cut the racial tension with a knife, especially when driving through rural towns. One incident I specifically remember happened in the North at the Carrier Dome in Syracuse, New York. As I was walking down one of those monstrous hills to my rental car, I heard yelling behind me from a disappointed Syracuse fan, who had just witnessed his home team lose a Big East game. Soon, the muffled yelling got clearer and clearer. As I looked back, I realized it was coming from a tall white man, who

---

[24] Derrick Bryson Taylor. "A St. John's Fencing Coach is Fired after Making Racist Remarks." *New York Times.* 13 Jun 2020.

weighed over 200 pounds. "I KNOW WHY WE LOST...'CAUSE WE HAVE A BUNCH OF LAZY NIGGERS PLAYING FOR US."

Needless to say, I was taken aback. I was the only black person in the vicinity as he walked in the crowd of orange shirts and white faces. Clearly, I was the target of his sounding board. I made sure I turned around, as I stood about 50 feet away. I knew he was trying to bait me into a confrontation, and he almost did. He went on to yell at some white children and their family that were walking across the street. "I FEEL SORRY FOR THOSE CHILDREN...CAUSE THEY GOTTA GROW UP WITH A NIGGER IN THE WHITE HOUSE." More bait for me to react, as he referred to President Obama.

I am pretty sure I might have punched him right in his face, had I not been there as a Brooklyn Nets employee. However, at that moment, I had to talk myself through the consequences as I continued to proceed to my car. I was outnumbered, and I saw no allies. No one in a huge sea of white people spoke up to quell his racist rants.

Though I am a big fan of the Black Panthers, the Deacons of Defense, and Malcolm X's approach, on this occasion I had to summon the discipline and nonviolent mindset of Dr. Martin Luther King and the SCLC. I took a deep breath, ignored the verbal abuse, and kept it moving. I had to let it go although, in a way, I will never let it go because it is an experience I will never forget.

When it comes to cultural or racial issues, the gift of a coach relating to a player does not end in college. For example, I am sure that black players in the NBA have no problem running through the symbolic "brick wall" for white coaches like George Popovich of the San Antonio Spurs and Steve Kerr of the Golden State Warriors. Both have spoken against former President Donald Trump consistently during his overtly racist tenure. Coach Popovich stated recently, "Especially if you're a white coach and you're coaching a group that's largely black, you'd better gain their trust, you'd better be genuine, you'd better understand their situation," (*Tampa Bay Times* by Times news services).

Well said Coach Popovich... You get it!!

When I evaluate college coaching staffs, I am leery of a white head coach whose staff is all white in a sport that features so many black players. A coach's staff includes bench coaches, managers, strength/ fitness coaches, medical staff, video production and administration personnel. John Calipari, the Hall of Fame head coach of Kentucky, asked this in the article in *The Undefeated* titled, "Where are the black coaches in the power conferences?": "When you look at your staff of people, who have you hired? How do you make those decisions?" These are my thoughts, when one of my players is being recruited.

The head coach's staff is a reflection of himself. Our children need to be in a healthy situation where they feel free to talk about issues that come up, that go beyond the sport they are playing. I am referring to racism, poverty, health issues, gender, and so forth. Typically, a black athlete will speak more candidly with a black coach than with anyone else, just as female athletes are typically more comfortable talking to female coaches. While there are white coaches who are sensitive and empathetic to the issues of their black players, given the option, black student athletes usually will seek out a coach or staff member who they feel can relate to them.

For many of our black athletes, their freshman year in college is the first time that they have been away from home. Suddenly, many young athletes are in an environment that does not look like their community. "Black men make up only 2.4 percent of the total under-graduate population of the 65 schools in the so-called Power Five athletic conferences."[25] How does that dynamic affect black athletes? Do they feel isolated? Do they feel pressure to assimilate? Is there anxiety that has been suppressed?

Often, the elite black athlete is surrounded by white handlers, agents and financial planners, figures whom they do not see in their own communities. A young brother from Brooklyn going to play at

---

[25] Jemele Hill. "It's Time for Black Athletes to Leave White Colleges." *The Atlantic.* 9 Sep 2019.

a school in Kentucky or Louisiana might deal with cultural differences that can be overwhelming. The political dynamics of different states and their agendas trickle down from college presidents to the students. At times, the policies can, be shocking from a cultural standpoint. Most student-athletes never think of these issues when choosing a school. Therefore, it is up to a parent or mentor to educate themselves on these issues so they can inform their children.

CHAPTER 11

HBCU FACTOR

I n 1987, Bill Cosby created a sitcom spin-off of his hit television show *The Cosby Show*. I was a fourteen-year-old high school freshman when I first watched A *Different World*. Both programs, were on the limited list of television shows that my mother would allow me to watch. She was very conscious of what I consumed as my daily food for thought.

As a single black woman with a black son, my mother represented the first line of defense for my psyche and self-esteem. She was consciously aware of the negative images and messages that I would be bombarded with in this country. My mother knew that my vulnerable mindset would be infiltrated with the false narratives of everything black was bad/wrong and everything white was right. "The black cat," the "black market," and the "black sheep of the family" all come with negative connotations. She knew one day my critical mind would ask why Jesus was white.

Dr. Martin Luther King, Jr. addressed racist language in a speech years before I was born:

"Somebody told a lie one day. They couched it in language. They made everything black ugly and evil. Look in your dictionary and see the synonyms of the word 'black.' It is always something degrading, low, and sinister. Look at the word 'white.' It's always something pure, high, clean."

My lioness mother was protective of her cub's mind. Thus, *The Cosby Show* and the positive images it created were approved, as was A *Different World*. As Dr. Neil Postman states,

"Although language is heard on television, and sometimes assumes importance, it is the practice that dominates the viewer's consciousness and carries the critical meanings. To say it as simple as one can, people watch television. They do not read it. Nor do they much listen to it. They watch it. This is true of adults and children, intellectuals and laborers, fools and wise men."

Every week, I was fixated on A *Different World*'s fictional Hillman College, which featured young, educated brothers and sisters at an all-black college. Their stories were hilarious and thought-provoking but, most of all, relatable. I dreamed of going to a college like Hillman, filled with brothers I could hang out with and, of course, introduce myself to fine-ass sisters like Whitley Gilbert, played by Jasmine Guy, or Kim Reese, played by Charnele Brown.

My mother and father, although divorced, remained friends and, three years later, planned a family college tour to black schools in the South with my cousins, Rahiem and Luqman, and my best friend Martin. We packed up the minivan with ice, drinks, cold cuts, and snacks. I can still hear Public Enemy's, "Brothers Gonna Work It Out" blaring from the speakers while the tape cassette played. Chuck D's booming voice roared through our windows:

> So many of us in limbo
> How to get it on, it's quite simple
> Three stones from the sun
> We need a piece of this rock
> Our goal indestructible soul
> Answers to this quizzing
> To the Brothers in the street
> Schools and the prisons
> History shouldn't be a mystery
> Our stories real history
> Not his story

The crew and I visited Norfolk University, Hampton University, North Carolina A&T, North Carolina Central, Clark University, Morris Brown, and Morehouse College. After that tour, there was no question that I was going to go to a black college.

As soon as I walked on campus, I felt at home. I was in a mini-Africa for students. If Morehouse was mini-Africa, then we thought Spelman College was heaven. We saw inspired, motivated, educated, and beautiful sisters of all complexions and body types. Whatever you preferred as a brother, Spelman had it on deck. Spelman was the ultimate hook that led me to eventually choose Morehouse, since they are across the street from each other and are both the educational incubators for so many successful black professionals all over the country. Not to mention that Morehouse is the very institution where Dr. Martin Luther King and Spike Lee walked the halls. After graduating from Morehouse College and becoming a coach, I made sure that my players were aware that going to an HBCU needed to be one of their options in the pursuit of becoming college bound student-athletes.

It amazes me that so many of us have forgotten or were not aware that there was a time when HBCUs had the wealth of athletic talent. It was not too long ago when black people were not allowed to attend the same schools as white people. This was during Jim Crow and segregation when it was prohibited by law for black people to even drink from a WHITES ONLY water fountain.

The South was slowest to integrate their educational institutions.

> "Integration also stopped a growing momentum toward independence and self-definition within the African American community. Prior to integration, many southern born African American athletes were forced to attend HBCUs that were close to their homes. This created a family like atmosphere surrounding black schools, they were as much a part of the community as were the families themselves."

—Bill Rhoden, *Forty Million Dollar Slaves*

In 1966, the University of Kentucky had an all-white roster in their competition against Texas Western, which featured an all-black starting line-up. That was the first time in an NCAA basketball championship game that the black/white dynamic was so stark. Texas Western beat Kentucky 72-65. The University of Kentucky, remarkably, integrated their athletic program three years after their devastating loss.

When choosing a college, I strongly urge the black athlete to become more informed about the HBCU college experience. I am aware that the Five-Star athlete might want to go to the blue blood schools, such as Kansas, Kentucky, Duke, or North Carolina. I am not naïve, the facilities are nicer, the exposure is better, and their track record of NBA players is well recorded. I have respect for the sports credentials of all those institutions.

However, in my time as an NBA scout with the Nets, I evaluated players in some of the most inconspicuous places. It was my job to go find the prospect wherever he might be. I left no stone unturned, and neither did most NBA scouts I know. I have been to junior colleges, Division II schools and, yes, historically black colleges.

Recent NBA players who have come from HBCU schools includes All-NBA First-Team defensive player and three-point shooting specialist, Robert Covington who went undrafted out of Tennessee State in 2013. "Going to an HBCU, it's just a different aspect, a different understanding of things and you are immersed in a different culture compared to what other universities may offer," Covington said.

In 2012, I went to the MEAC conference to scout such teams as Howard University, North Carolina A&T, North Carolina Central, and Norfolk University. I was at the Norfolk game specifically to scout a six-foot-eight, rugged-playing big man with good hands and decent feet. His name was Kyle O'Quinn, and he did not disappoint. He had close to a double-double against Howard in the quarterfinal game.

Norfolk went on to win the tournament, before upsetting Number 3 seed University of Missouri in the NCAA Tournament.

Kyle finished the game with 26 points and fourteen rebounds in 37 minutes. About a month later, I went to the Portsmouth Invitational Tournament, which is a postseason showcase event for college seniors. I saw Kyle play again. He outran, out-hustled, and out-re-bounded most of the 'bigs' he competed against at the showcase. He played with the hunger of an unfed wolf.

He was awarded the MVP of Portsmouth over a bunch of players who came from more recognizable schools, including Georgetown, Florida, Syracuse, and UNLV. Kyle performed and showed up when the lights were brightest. He was drafted in the second round of the 2012 NBA Draft, as the 49th pick by the Orlando Magic. The Nets did not draft him but, after doing his intel and meeting him in person during our interviews, I began rooting for him from afar. I was proud that he went to an HBCU and grinded his way into the NBA. That is a helluva story for someone who had had only one scholarship offer in his senior year, coming out of Campus Magnet High School in Queens, New York. Other notable HBCU/NBA alumni include Willis Reed from Grambling State, Rick Mahorn from Hampton University, Ben Wallace and Charles Oakley from Virginia Union, as well as leg-endary Knick Earl Monroe of Winston-Salem State.

Many NBA players have come out of the traditional mid-major schools as well. In 1996, the six-foot-eleven, slimly built Marcus Camby was the second pick in the draft out of the University of Massachusetts. More recently, the elite scorer Stephen Curry was the seventh overall pick out of Davidson in 2009. CJ McCollum of the New Orleans Pelicans was the tenth pick in the 2013 NBA draft, out of Lehigh University in Pennsylvania. None of these schools have the same resources as the University of Connecticut, Duke University, or UCLA. However, after being under the radar for most of their careers, all of these players created their own buzz before becoming stars in the NBA.

The same formula can be used if a player attends a black college. As mentioned earlier, before black people were allowed to play for any white college, the best players played for black institutions. At that time, I'm sure presidents and athletic directors from white universities could not have imagined the money that black athletes would gross for their universities and conferences post-segregation. For HBCUs to attract big name athletes, money must be poured into the athletic budgets of these black universities.

Donations from high-profile NBA players who have expressed verbal support for black athletes attending HBCUs, can make an impact with a donation. What if celebrities, such as noted basketball fan Jay-Z, would get behind the cause? It would change the game overnight.

In 2017, the NCAA reported $1.1 billion for the fiscal year. Most of the money comes from the Division I men's NCAA basketball tournament. In 2016, the NCAA extended its television agreement with CBS Sports and Turner Broadcasting through the year 2032— an $8.8 billion deal. About 30 Division I schools bring in at least $100 million each in athletic revenue every year. Almost all of these schools are majority white; yet, black men make up 55 percent of the football players from those schools and 56 percent of the basketball players. With these numbers in mind, we would not be dis- cussing a lack of resources at black universities if some of our elite players chose to attend them.

Recently, I had the honor of meeting with nineteen-year-old 5-Star recruit Makur Maker during an ABIS zoom call. He made a big splash by committing to play at Howard University over historical powerhouses UCLA and Kentucky. He credits his high school coach for planting the seed to play at an HBCU. Maker stated,

"My interest in Howard started during the [2017-18] high school basketball season. I already had offers from some of the top schools in the country, but my coach pulled me aside one day and said, 'why don't you think about Howard.'"

Maker went on to describe his visit to Howard's campus, stating,

> *"One of the first things that went through my mind as I walked around was, 'this feels like family.' Black people like me for as far as you could see. Black people—students and alumni—all doing great things. Highly motivated people, successful people, and I tried to talk to as many of them as I could because I wanted to pick everybody's brain. The main thing I felt being there: the collective culture. Everyone knew every- one's name, everyone was connected, everyone had ambitions or was pursuing something in life. And that was really appealing to me.*[26]

In 2018, Howard University spent $4,795,237 on men's teams and received $5,497,958 in revenue. That is $94 million less than what is generated by Division I universities in the Big 5 conferences. Maker eventually played one season at Howard. He is now playing professionally in Australia.

In the 2007-2008 season, Davidson College head coach, Bob McKillop, had the same line of thinking when he placed his college superstar Stephen Curry on a national stage. He booked non-conference games against the University of North Carolina, Duke and UCLA, all of whom were all ranked in the top fifteen in the country at one point. Curry did the rest of the work on the national stage.

At Long Island University, when I was on coach Ray Haskins's staff, our star player, Charles Jones, thrived under our "run and gun" system. He became the leading scorer in the nation, averaging 30 points per game. Coach deliberately set up a national non-conference schedule. We went on to play against the University of Minnesota, St. John's University (whom we beat), Providence College, Ohio State

---

[26] Jerry Bembry. "Top hoops recruit Makur Maker chooses Howard in a game-changer for HBCUs." *The Undefeated.* 9 Jul 2020.

University, and Xavier University. Charles performed well in these games, and LIU received money for its appearances.

HBCU football programs often play against some of the "big boy" institutions to accept "ass kickings" for money.

Southern University collected $650,000 to play Georgia in 2015. They lost 48-6. In 2017, Howard University pulled off an upset against UNLV in Las Vegas. They went into the game as a 45-point under-dog but, instead, won 43-40. Howard's participation in the game also poured $650,000 into the coffers of their athletic department. The Bison athletic director said the money "is helpful... Institutions that are what people consider lower-resource institutions have histori-cally needed games like this to help with their operating budget."[27]

What if Makur had become the number five pick of the draft? How would that help the Howard brand in the future? How much excitement did his commitment generate on Howard's campus, which is known typically for its ambience, brotherhood, sisterhood, and culture?

Going forward, our community's well-to-do should invest in the athletic departments of Howard and other HBCUs. The financial help would put some HBCU facilities on par with those of white institutions. In the summer of 2019, Stephen Curry gave Howard a seven-figure donation to fund their men's and women's Division I golf programs.

In contrast, in 2003, Carmelo Anthony donated $3 million to kick-start a fund-raising campaign for a new basketball practice complex at Syracuse University, called The Carmelo K. Anthony Basketball Center. This building is a clean, state of the art, 54,000 square foot structure that features two NCAA regulation-size courts made of first-grade maple, with coaching suites, a study room, and weight training rooms. I have watched numerous practices in this building. I

---

[27] Adam Kilgore. "Why was Howard playing UNLV anyway? It wasn't just college football as usual." *The Washington Post.* 8 Sep 2017.

must say, it is impressive and comparable to an NBA facility. According to Syracuse.com: "In the five years since the Melo Center opened, Syracuse has brought in four McDonald's All-Americans and sent five players to the NBA." What a recruiting tool! As we know, Melo led Syracuse to a National Championship as a freshman in 2003 and earned Most Outstanding Player of the tournament.

"[The] Men's basketball tournament basically funds the NCAA's existence. Between television revenue and ticket sales, the tournament annually produces more than $700 million. The NCAA keeps about 40 percent and distributes the remaining 60 percent to schools; the basketball fund is the largest piece of that distribution." For example, thanks to its Final Four run, "[the university] earned an estimated $8.33 million, which is the maximum for most teams."[28]

A few months later, Anthony was drafted as the number three pick in the NBA Draft. His presence also impacted Carrier Dome ticket sales, concessions, and merchandise sales. What a return on Syracuse's investment! Can you imagine if Anthony had produced that same amount of long-lasting success at Delaware State or Bethune Cookman? HBCUs need that same financial boost.

The MEAC (Mid-East Athletic Conference) recently showed signs of stepping into the modern era of college sports when they dropped their uniform deal with Russell Athletics, which they had had since 2004. No disrespect to Russell, but their uniforms are not a good sell for young athletes who have been playing on Nike, Adidas, or Under

Armour circuits and receiving free gear. Recently, Howard University entered into a 20-year deal with the Jordan Brand. They will be provided shoe and athletic wear.

The elite talent coming out of our 'hoods' is like precious diamonds or gold that must be taken care of and maintained. Black/brown student-athletes must be educated on how their school decisions

---

28 Will Hobson. "Fun and Games." *The Washington Post*. 18 Mar 2014.

can help their people as a whole. They must be educated to look at their decisions from a holistic standpoint that includes economics.

There is an old saying in sports that there is no "I" in team. The team that black/brown athletes need to keep in mind is the team from where they came. It won't be easy, and they need to begin to think from a communal, not an individual, perspective. While they weigh the pros and cons of their decisions, they must keep in mind that Black Dollars Matter.

An elite black player's decision to choose an HBCU would be just as impactful as Colin Kaepernick heroically taking a knee. Maker said he "wanted to change the culture" when he discussed his decision. For some reason, I think this is the beginning of a revolution in the minds of our athletes, and I am all for it. Makur Maker stated in a tweet, "I hope I inspire guys like Mikey Williams to join me on this journey."

Mikey Williams, a six-foot-two guard from California, is one of the top basketball prospects in the class of 2023. He stated: "When that time does come that I have to narrow my schools down to whatever number it is . . . there WILL be multiple HBCUs on that list! And they won't just be there for show." Williams is a big-time prospect, but he is also very popular in the social media world. He has over 3.5 million followers, including the rapper Drake, LeBron James, and Kevin Durant. Mikey has recently skipped the college process altogether. He signed with Excel Sports Management and is set to make millions of dollars with his name, image, and likeness.

Carmelo Anthony also backed the notion of black youth attending HBCUs. Before Maker made his commitment, Anthony stated: "All it takes is one person to change history," in a video posted to Instagram.

"I think it's a better chance of this next generation to go to an HBCU and be accepted and bring something different to an HBCU, as opposed to what was happening in 2002. So, do I think a kid like Mikey

Williams should consider an HBCU? I think he should based on the power he has within himself. If he does that, it changes college sports because you have a young, black kid who is at the top of his game, who decides to go to a black university, that's totally different."[29]

As part of the 2022 All-Star festivities in Cleveland, Ohio, the NBA featured an HBCU Classic as Morgan State played Howard University. This gave these schools a big platform for both promotion of their respective universities and recruitment of student athletes who normally might not be paying attention.

As black people, it does not make any sense for our most elite resources to be marketed, advised, and managed by people who do not always have our best interests in mind. You do not see the greatest assets of the Jewish community marketed, advised, and managed by black people. You also do not see the Asian community gullibly allowing everyone other than their own people to reap benefits off their greatest assets. So, why shouldn't we as black people think in similar terms?

Some of the best professional black minds have come from the HBCU community. Seventeen percent of all bachelor's degrees and 24 percent of all STEM-related bachelor's degrees earned by black students in the United States were conveyed by HBCUs, according to a 2019 report. HBCUs also supply more black applicants to medical schools than non–HBCU institutions. And HBCUs have graduated 40 percent of all black engineers; 40 percent of all black US Congress members; 50 percent of all black lawyers; and 80 percent of all black judges.[30]

Of the degrees conferred by HBCUs in 2017-18, the majority (74 percent) were to black students. Black students earned 43 percent of the 5,500 associate degrees, 81 percent of the 32,600 bachelor's

[29] Jeff Borzello. "Why HBCUs could again become serious options for elite basketball prospects." ESPN. 25 Jun 2020.
[30] Bevins, Frankki; Fox, Kathryn; Pinder, Duwain; Sarakatsannis, Jimmy; Stewart, Shelley. "HBCUs as engines of black economic mobility." McKinsey & Co. 30 Jul 2021.

degrees, 71 percent of the 7,700 master's degrees, and 62 percent of the 2,500 doctorate degrees.

In modern day sports, LeBron James is a great example of an athlete who has exercised one of the principles of Kwanzaa: Kujichacalia or Self-Determination. When LeBron first entered the NBA, he was represented by two black agents, Aaron and Eric Goodwin. They negotiated sponsorship deals that totaled over $135 million in U.S. endorsement deals, including $90 million from his Nike contract.

In 2005, LeBron fired the Goodwin brothers and, instead, chose to be managed by his inner circle, which included Randy Mihms, James's personal assistant and road manager. LeBron is now represented by his longtime friend, Rich Paul, another black man, who started Klutch Sports. Paul soon leveraged his relationship with LeBron to sign NBA stars Anthony Davis, Eric Bledsoe, John Wall, Ben Simmons, and Draymond Green. LeBron also empowered his high school teammate, Maverick Carter. Carter has served as James's business manager since 2006. Prior to that, he was a Nike field rep. Along with James, Paul, and Randy Mims, he is one of the founders of LRMR, their sports marketing company.

Carter was responsible for engineering *The Decision*, a television special. LeBron must get big credit for "Doing for self," or as the Honorable Marcus Garvey once stated, "The Negro will have to build his own industry, art, sciences, literature, and culture before the world will stop to consider him." "The King" valued himself enough to know that he did not have to look outside of his community or brotherhood to develop a long-lasting influence on the sports industry.

LeBron James has created generational wealth for his family and his community. He chose to control his own destiny, as I implore up-and-coming athletes and their parents to do. Again, we have professional geniuses within our communities, whose potential needs to be tapped. There are no more excuses—unless a parent or player is suffering from mental slavery. The mental chains that make you think the "white man's ice is colder" than your own, or that their vision for your life is more credible, must be discarded.

CHAPTER 12

PROTECT YOUR PLAYER, PROTECT YOURSELF
NURTURE YOUR CHARACTER/
PROTECT YOUR REPUTATION

E arly on, as I began evaluating talent for the New Jersey Nets, I was not aware of all the details scouting would encompass. For example, a real shot-maker shoots with efficiency. Most college players are inherently athletic; however, only certain players are exceptionally explosive finishers at the rim.

I developed a higher appreciation for rebounders and learned that there is a big difference between pulling down rebounds in traffic or outside of a player's area. When looking specifically at centers, close attention must be paid to a big man's run strides. My late mentor, Bob Ferry, who was once the general manager for the Baltimore Bullets and who won an NBA championship in 1978, taught me the importance of having good hands as well as good feet. Bob was my favorite travel buddy on the road. He was a white man who did not shy away from having conversations with me about any topics including matters of race in America. He also had one of the best senses of humor I have ever come across. I truly miss my elder comrade in the game.

After picking the brains of more experienced scouts and assistant general managers, I learned quickly that my original approach to scouting was naive and unseasoned. I now understand that one of the most important elements of scouting is to collect "intel" and do background checks. As a scout, it was my job to make sure my supervisors, who included the director of Player Development, assistant general manager, general manager, and head coach, were equipped with as much information as possible regarding a prospect. I was provided a format and guide that I could use to ask questions that would stimulate conversations. After spending an entire year evaluating a player, it could be very disappointing when the intel did not coincide with the athlete's physical ability.

I spent countless hours calling different sources I had accumulated in my Rolodex throughout my years in the game. My sources would include a player's former team managers, AAU coaches, current and former coaches, academic advisors, athletic trainers, strength coaches, or just a brother from their hood. Sometimes, I would call six or seven different references regarding one player.

I would think often about a prospect's developmental years; so many lacked stability at home. The players who were not held accountable in their homes often lacked humility. Many of the players lacked self-awareness and thought they were better than they really were due to having too many "yes" men or women in their lives. When asking about a player's family background, I wanted to know about their parents' professions and inquired about their siblings and friends. I asked about the player's personality: was he an introvert or extrovert?

It was my job to ask my sources how the prospect handled success or failure. Does he love the game, or does he love the benefits that come with the game? Does he have a strong passion to play? Is he punctual and reliable? Has he had any major injuries? Has he had any major surgeries? Can he remember plays or make quick adjustments in the game? Is he a leader? If so, what is his leadership style? Is he mentally or physically tough? Who in the NBA can we compare him to? Is he a drug user or alcohol drinker? How are his practice habits? Is he a gym rat? Who is the main influence in his life? Who would come live with him if we were to draft him?

Parent or player, you should look at some of the above questions. As an athlete, it is important to be aware of the character you are projecting because it can cost you or help you. This does not only pertain to potential draft picks, but to anyone. As a player, you should protect your reputation as if you are your own corporation. It is up to you to define and control your own narrative, or rest assured *someone else will.* Believe me, the basketball world is smaller than it looks. There might be fewer than six degrees of separation for AAU, high school, college coaches, and NBA personnel. I have worn all those hats, so I value all their perspectives.

I have been in meetings where the deciding factor between two evenly talented players came down to the intel that was collected. In fact, most times when a prospect who was once highly ranked drops in a draft, it is due to a "red flag" in his medical record or background intel. My general manager and/or director of scouting would ask if we thought the prospect's risk was worth the reward. This means the player had better be bringing something valuable to the table that is unique from other players, or it is not worth drafting him.

The risk/reward factor also has a lot to do with where a team is drafting a player; the lower in the draft a player is picked, the less is paid in salary. Also, NBA contracts are not guaranteed in the second round, so if that player does something stupid to embarrass the franchise, he will be easier to cut. Obviously, the risk/ reward factor can pertain to all players regardless of level.

When Kyle Neptune was the assistant coach at the University of Villanova, he told me that legendary head coach Jay Wright prefers to recruit talented, high character, low maintenance players. Those are the only players who fit into the national championship basketball culture that he and his staff have built.

When I coached at Bishop Loughlin High School, I was willing to take a "risk kid" every now and then, as long as the boy was ready to make adjustments. In Brooklyn, New York, it was common to coach talented players with dysfunctional backgrounds. In fact, some of the most talented players I coached had serious issues.

A father's absence in the household always seemed to be a prevailing theme. These boys usually lacked some level of discipline and structure. Their mothers did the best they could to raise them but, at some point in their childhood, it was not enough. Maybe deep inside, I loved the challenge of working with these young brothers. Like them, I reached an age where I began to tune out my mother's voice. And, like them, I did things growing up that were risky and tainted my character. As their coach, I could relate and wanted to help them avoid those mistakes.

It is important that parents keep the right people around their children during the developmental years. The character of the people in your child's life can either hurt or help their growth. I have often told my players, "If you show me your friends, I'll show you who you are. Your circle is a reflection of you." Make sure your children roll or hang with 'the winners'!

NAME, IMAGE, LIKENESS

In 1995, Edward O' Bannon won Most Outstanding Player of the Men's Basketball NCAA Championship for UCLA. In 2009, he filed a lawsuit against College Licensing Company and the NCAA for using his likeness on the EA Sport title without his permission. Can you imagine seeing a video image of you in a game with the same uniform, same height, exact uniform number and color, and yet you were not told your image would be used to gain profit? O'Bannon won the case in 2014, which has since changed the landscape of college sports and amateur athletics in general.

Ironically as well as hypocritically, the NCAA officially lists itself as a nonprofit organization. However, the presidents of universities, the Entertainment and Sports Programming Network (ESPN), as well as all the local "mom and pop" businesses surrounding these institutions have accumulated generational wealth on the backs of black and brown student athletes who are elite at playing sports. Football and basketball programs generate the most revenue on college campuses. Almost half of all college football players are black while black student athletes make up over half of the basketball population. On the other hand, many student athletes come from impoverished communities and, up until this point, were not able to receive legal compensation for their work on the field or the court. In Article 12 of the NCAA By Laws, it states "only an amateur student athlete is eligible for intercollegiate participation in a particular sport."

As of July 1, 2021, due to NCAA rule changes as well as new state laws, student athletes can now monetize their social media accounts, participate in advertising campaigns, and sign autographs, among other potential undertakings. Many student athletes have already begun to cash in. For example, UCLA 2023 commit Jada Williams, whom I interviewed on my Upnext Podcast, recently joined Spalding's Ambassador program. Also, basketball phenom Mikey Williams, whom I mentioned earlier in this book, has more than five million followers between Instagram, TikTok and Twitter. Recently, he cashed in on his popularity by signing a multi-year deal with Puma.

Inevitably, for grammar school to high school children and parents the lure to cash in on their fame will be enticing. It will be important that black and brown parents in particular set up the proper infrastructure that will help their children navigate the NIL journey. The history of the exploitation of black and brown people by human bloodsuckers in the sports and entertainment industries in this country is long. They will need to surround themselves with people who will genuinely guard their best interests. Recently, schools in the Catholic League in New York City have partnered wisely with companies to teach their youth about brand building and marketing. This is a new day in youth sports and knowledge is power. Understanding the developing ecosystem can lead to a clear mental picture, resulting in healthy marketing and financial decisions.

CHOOSING THE RIGHT AGENT

Choosing the right agent is not as simple as it sounds. Similar to choosing a school or coach, this decision should be based on the individual needs of the athlete. I have seen non-elite players choose an agent based on the branding of the particular agency. Sometimes, the bigger the agency, the worse the situation is for the player.

If you are not a high-profile prospect, you might not get the attention you desire. However, during my years in the NBA, I have also witnessed that the more high-profile clients an agent has, the more leverage he will possess to help lesser profile prospects around the league. Favors are done all the time based on an agent's cache. I have seen agents imply to teams that their big-name clients might sign with a particular team if their lesser name client is taken care of; hence, the leverage provides a lesser-known prospect a spot in training camp or on a summer league team.

In the beginning of the process, agents will start to follow a player as the player's name emerges on the radar. Some agents have the means, resources, and savvy to lock into players earlier than others. In the NBA, powerful agents can get players traded where they want to go. Some are also known to have great relationships with journalists, making them able to place "stories" that work in their client's interest. Proactive agents will bond with family members as well as grassroots directors, coaches, and handlers to get an edge over their competitors. Ultimately, a seasoned agent will also do their homework regarding who the player is, on and off the court, to gauge if the potential client is worth the investment in time and resources.

If you are a big-time prospect, you will be viewed as an investment. The agent might come with a financial planner who could use an AAU program or a mentor as a conduit to get money to the player. In interviews with Hoops Hype, one anonymous agent stated, "I'd say the vast majority of players who are in the draft conversation are taking money from agents, sometimes while they're still in school." Another agent said:

"I'd say somewhere between 75 percent and 90 percent of players get paid. Sometimes, it's the player taking money. Sometimes, it's a family member and, in those cases, it may be unbeknownst to the player. Certain agents have a reputation for paying players or their relatives while they're still in school."

These transactions, if revealed, could jeopardize a player's amateur status, put the college the player attends in a legally/ethically vulnerable position, and the agent could be liable as well.

It is common knowledge that a lot of players will have an idea who their agent is going to be while still in high school. If the player is big-time, then he will most likely get paid a "retainer fee" in high school. I know of certain situations where agents have influenced where an eighth grader goes to high school. Some agents have had previous relationships with high school coaches and, thus, there is an incentive for the player to go to a particular high school.

Big-time prospects often get money through multiple sources because, until they sign, they are not beholden to anyone. At a certain point, a prospect and their inner circle will sit down for a meeting with the agent, where the agent will make a pitch. The pitch will sound something like this:

- What they can do for you
- How they are different from the other agencies
- They will likely take a jab at other agencies if you happen to bring them up.
- Talk about how they can get sponsorships for you.
- How they can help you in your post-playing days

A parent's role and a prospect's job is to listen, observe, and do your research. You must be in control of the whole process. As I have said over and over again in this book: know your value and negotiate from a place of strength. You do not have to sign at the first agent meeting if you are not ready. You might not want to sign until after the second or third meeting. That is okay.

Remember, this is a business. Similar to being recruited by an AAU program, high school or college, you are talking to a salesman. Therefore, take notes or have someone from your inner circle keep a record of what is said for later reference. You might want to ask if you can tape the meeting. This is not only to hold the agent accountable for their pitch, but also so you can compare what is being offered by the other agents with whom you will be meeting. It will help you as you consider the pros and cons of the agents you meet.

Ask how the potential agent is doing with other players that he/she represents, both current and past clients. The agent might have a client who is similar to you as a player. If so, they might be able to project and speak to your career trajectory. In my opinion, it would be beneficial for the agent you choose to have an array of young, seasoned, and veteran clients. Then, you would be able to get a realistic perspective of where you could be as your professional career progresses.

If you are a potential NBA Draft pick, an agency will have a comprehensive plan for your pre-draft workouts and training. Before the meeting, do your research regarding your own stock and where teams might want to draft you. At the meeting, ask what your stock in the draft is. Here is a chance to see if the agent will tell you the truth or sugarcoat the projection. If you are a low-profile player, you need to assess where the agent places his players. For example, if you are an overseas prospect, it is your job to make sure he can get you placed in quality leagues.

Over the years, I have gotten many calls from former college players who were dissatisfied with their agents for various reasons; but one of the most common is broken promises. Prospects did not do extensive preliminary homework, while others overestimated their own skill set.

While the NBA has the best competition in the world, there are other leagues, such as the Euro League, Spain's Liga ACB, The Turkish Basketball Super League, and Russia's VTB United League. They are all highly competitive. There are international leagues also that are known for not paying on time or simply not paying enough. Do your research! It would be wise to have an agent who specializes in the international market if that is your destiny. Below are suggested questions to ask your agent:

- Why do you want to sign me?
- What is your marketing plan for me?
- Who else do you represent?
- What is the proudest moment in your career as an agent?
- How can you help my post-playing plans?
- Can you guarantee I get paid on time? If so, how?

You might come up with more questions. Feel free to add on and be bold enough to be an advocate for yourself.

EAT TO LIVE/HEALTH IS WEALTH

In more than twenty years of experience in basketball, I have coached and been around black and brown children from all over the country. I have met so many student athletes on the national AAU circuit, in national camps, as well as on college campuses. It is well documented that many of these children live in food deserts.

What is a food desert? A food desert is usually in a 'ghetto' or a 'hood.' While the term ghetto is a word that usually refers to certain black and brown communities, some poor white people reside in the hood as well. The word ghetto was highlighted in 1939 when Nazi forces established the first ghetto in Poland for its Jewish citizens. These ghettos were the most rundown areas of a city. Like today's ghettos, Jews lived in overcrowded spaces, food was scarce, and living conditions were miserable. Does this sound familiar?

Typically, food deserts are in an area where the local gas station or corner store bodega sells food that has no nutritional value. What is offered instead are salt and vinegar potato chips, Tropical Fantasy juices, Corn Nuts, Little Debbies, Sour Patches, bacon egg and cheese, Gummy Bears, and the like. Simply put, JUNK FOOD!

As of 2019, the top food deserts in the country were located in these cities:

- New York City, New York
- Atlanta, Georgia
- Detroit, Michigan
- Chicago, Illinois
- San Francisco, California
- Seattle, Washington
- Camden, New Jersey
- New Orleans, Louisiana
- Minneapolis, Minnesota
- Memphis, Tennessee

Ann Casano wrote in an article in *Ranker* on July 19, 2019:

"In 2008 the NY City Department of City Planning found that 3 million city residents live in a food desert. Also, from 2000 to 2014, there was a sharp rise in the presence of fast-food restaurants across New York, particularly in Brooklyn...[in the Bronx] most residents are forced to shop at local corner stores with a very limited selection of fresh vegetables and fruit. Black people are also more likely to live in areas without clean water or air. African Americans are more likely to live near landfills and industrial plants that pollute water and air and erode quality of life. Because of this, more than half of the 9 million people living near hazardous waste sites are people of color, and black Americans are three times more likely to die from exposure to air pollutants than their white counterparts."

Five years ago, we learned the residents of Flint, Michigan, were drinking poisonous tap water. Flint has 53 percent black residents and has one of the highest poverty rates in the country. Residents residing in the Bronx suffer from the highest rate of deaths from diabetes in all of NYC. It is common knowledge that those who live in food deserts are susceptible to high obesity rates as well. According to the CDC, Hispanics have a 25.6 percent obesity rate, while blacks are at 24.2 percent. and among non-Hispanic white children the rate is 16.1 percent. Why are there such disparities between these communities? I think it's obvious, but here are the actual facts.

We need to look no further than *redlining*, which is precisely the act of systematically marking off specific zones/neighborhoods and is a form of institutional racism. According to Jonathan Burdick's article "Tracing Erie's History of Redlining," dated February 13, 2019, "redlining policies were intentional in deciding what groups of people would be considered poor financial risks: Black families and immigrants." The term redlining was extended later to refer to the discriminatory practice of denying, or simply charging more for services to particular groups of people, such as banking insurance, HEALTH CARE or FOOD at supermarkets.

After WWII, federal policies were created to offer veterans funding under the GI Bill. Black GIs were denied most of the benefits. However, under President Franklin Roosevelt's administration, the Homeowners Loan Corporation and the Federal Housing Administration agencies directed government guaranteed loans to white homeowners and away from non-whites.

Hence, the hood as we know it, is redlined (rated the lowest), which is a biased appraisal system of real estate in a community. White people received the green label for the highest rating. "The maps caused brokers to deny residents new thirty-year mortgages and prevented Black renters from purchasing a home and acquiring wealth." (Ibram X. Kendi, *Stamped from the Beginning*).

Redlining and zip codes, it seems, go hand in hand. Redlining or zip codes are just the descendants of segregation. As Nancy Updike states in *This American Life*, "Black and white Americans still live substantially apart in this country . . . In hundreds of metropolitan areas, the average white person lives in a neighborhood that's 75 percent white and the neighborhoods that aren't white are not likely to be African American."

As recently reported, "State by state, neighborhood by neighborhood, black families pay 13 percent more in property taxes each year than a white family would in the same situation."[31] The article cited a general contractor named Charles who had to leave his home in Chicago due to taxes. When speaking on the "Black tax" he stated, "It's almost like it's in the soil, it stretches all across the board. It's just not real estate. It's not just housing. It's not just food deserts. It's not just racism on the street. It's not just that you can't get a cab at night. It's just everything."

One's zip code affects everything, from the quality of education to the quality of the food that can be consumed from the local

---

[31] Andrew Van Dam. "Black families pay significantly higher property taxes." *The Washington Post*. 2 Jul 2020.

supermarket. Many years later, I realized that my mother was way ahead of the game. She was influenced by the jewels in the Honorable Elijah Muhammad's book titled, How to Eat to Live, as well as Dr. Sebi's teachings on food intake. I thought the way we ate at home was weird in comparison with my friends who were able to have soda, milk, pork and beef, foods that were non-starters in my home. When I competed in sports, my mother always had plenty of water, fruit, and granola bars on deck during my breaks.

Years later, as a coach and director of a program, contrary to my own upbringing, I have certainly been guilty of feeding myself and my players the typical "on the road" grub, such as McDonald's fries, pizza, chicken wings, potato chips, Gatorade and the like. As I have matured and my understanding of health has developed, I have become more conscious of what I buy for my players.

Now, on the road, I buy sandwiches from Subway or Jersey Mike's Subs. I urge our boys not to buy white bread, pork, bacon and sodas (though they don't always listen). It is hard to break some of their bad diet habits. So many of them eat certain foods based on access. Recently, these health inequities have shown their ugly face with COVID-19's emergence on the scene. During this pandemic, black Americans have been dying at about 2.4 times the rate of white Americans.

I remember vividly when the pandemic invaded my community. In about a ten-day span in March of 2020, I received calls and texts regarding brothers and sisters I knew who had died from the disease. People I coached against and brothers I watched excel playing basketball are no longer living; some mothers who were always with their children when I saw them walking around in the community are no longer around. The plague was on our heels, and we were all running from it with our gloves and masks on daily.

As essential workers, black and brown people in the U.S. are on the frontlines. We are bagging the groceries, driving the buses, serving as the corrections officers. Therefore, we are the most at risk, in a country that forces us to start our lives with limited options." The fact that the black body experiences so much more harm, in so many ways, compared to other bodies — it really explains how racism continues to hurt people," said Roberto Montenegro, a psychiatrist at Seattle Children's Hospital, who studies how perceived discrimination affects mental health.

When I worked with the Brooklyn Nets, I often called the athletic trainer and nutritionist of a college program to find out about the eating habits of a prospect I was scouting. Often, the nutritionist would tell me that an incoming freshman had to adjust to the healthy eating habits of a college student-athlete.

As stated earlier, poor eating patterns originate from the scarcity of healthy options in food deserts. But it is time our children made healthier choices when it comes to their food intake. Below are my dos and don'ts suggestions for proper student-athlete nutrition:

DOS:

- Drink plenty of water and stay hydrated (Start the morning by drinking water before consuming anything else.).
- Eat fish (but don't overeat it due to the mercury factor).
- Eat raw vegetables.
- Eat plenty of fruit.
- Consume honey instead of sugar.
- Drink hot water and lemon daily.
- Drink fresh blended juices and vegetables.

DON'TS

- Eat no dairy products that create mucus (e.g., eggs, cheese, milk)
- Eat pork, it causes high blood pressure.
- Eat chicken excessively.
- Eat white sugar products.
- Consume alcohol.
- Smoke marijuana.
- Take recreational prescription medicine.
- Drink soda.
- Eat fried food.
- Eat processed food.

Some may say that these suggestions are difficult to enforce in a child. I get it because I was hard-headed as a youth. My mother's regimen for me, which included a daily intake of cod liver oil and healthy fresh foods, ran contrary to what most of my peers were consuming. There is nothing sexy about smelling like fish from the cod liver oil in a school environment so, eventually, my sink got plenty of it instead of my mouth!!

I would not urge any parent to take on all these suggestions at once. However, I think some of these changes can be introduced slowly into the mindset of young people, particularly young athletes. I would urge parents to adopt the recent healthy changes in lifestyle that NBA players have adjusted to for their own children.

Twelve-time NBA All-Star, Chris Paul, recently embraced a plant-based diet.

"I do feel really good right now [he said after giving the diet change a try]. I think the biggest change for me is the aches and pains of the season. I started working out and training and I got to Monday, Tuesday and Wednesday and I thought, am I lifting hard enough? Am I training hard enough? Why am I not achy? There is a reason I try to eat the way I do and be as disciplined as possible."

Recently, Cade Cunningham, who was selected with the number one pick by the Detroit Pistons in the 2021 NBA Draft, stated he is a vegetarian. Like Chris Paul, I found out later in life that what my mother taught me about eating healthy was correct. Her goal was to prevent me from having to rely on doctors as I got older. She wanted me to be proactive with my health.

My mother was on to something. As Hippocrates, the so-called "Father of Medicine," stated: "Let food be thy medicine and medicine be thy food." Again, as an athlete, what you put into your body or your "engine," as well as what you don't put into it, is critical. Each day, we face a crossroads with our food intake and there is no middle ground. We either eat food that is going to build up the body or food that is going to slowly destroy it.

"The King," LeBron James, has an understanding. In my opinion, LeBron is one of the top three players in the history of the NBA game. Reportedly, he spends $1.5 million per year on his body. As his teammate Mike Miller once stated to *Bleacher Report*,

"Where a lot of people don't do it, [LeBron] puts a lot of money behind taking care of his body. A lot of people think it's a big expense, but that big expense has allowed him to make a lot more money for a long period of time."

LeBron is currently 37 years young, third in scoring in the NBA at 29 points per game, and played in his 18th All-Star game last season, tying Kobe Bryant and he is one All-Star game appearance behind Kareem Abdul Jabaar, for the most times participating in NBA history.

Of course, I know most, if not all, people reading this do not have the resources LeBron possesses. However, the first investment in our players' bodies begins with opening the mind. We can all start somewhere, why not now?

CHAPTER 13

PLAYING AND TRAINING

As a coach, I have found that there should be a healthy balance between training and playing. As co-director with the Juice All-Stars, a grassroots program started by the legendary NYC high school coach Dwayne "Tiny" Morton and sponsored by Adidas, I learned a lot from those who managed Sebastian "Bassy" Telfair when he was a rising junior. He was ranked as the top point guard in the nation, but he had so many people with their own agendas pulling him in different directions; so many people wanted him to attend their camps and/or national tournaments. His appearance at those events, like so many top athletes in their respective sports, added credibility to the event. What I admired about Sebastian and his camp was that they were very aware of his value.

His inner circle included his older brother, Jamel Thomas, who had a stellar career at Providence College and played overseas. His now-deceased older brother, Danny Turner, along with Dwayne "Tiny" Morton, also helped guide most of Bassy's decisions. In fact, they were really Bassy's first agents. They were very wise and selective when it came to choosing events and camps that made the most sense to support. They did not want to play without an ultimate purpose and wanted to maximize Bassy's time and efforts.

Tournaments, like the Big-Time tournament in Las Vegas, sponsored by Adidas, and the Kingwood Tournament in Texas, were musts for our Juice All-Star program, since we knew the top talent, ranking site publications, as well as journalists, would be in attendance. It was also mandatory that Bassy participate in camps such as ABCD and 5-Star Basketball Camp.

For an elite player like Sebastian, his incentive for attending 5-Star was to play in front of two now-deceased basketball legends: Howard Garfunkel, the founder, and Tom Konchalski, the top scout at the camp and, probably, in all high school sports. Both men were McDonald's All-American Game voters. Sebastian and his camp were aware that they had to show up at least once to the 5-Star Basketball Camp.

Again, the Telfair camp was very savvy, and they understood the politics of grassroots basketball. They also had the awareness to turn down frivolous tournaments that served no purpose for their ultimate agenda, which was to get Telfair to the NBA. They knew their value and they understood the game from a business perspective.

As I returned to coaching AAU in 2015, I walked into the new reality of the grassroots world. I noticed that from middle school down children were playing way too many games. For example, a team that competes in the championship game during an AAU weekend is going to play approximately four to six games, possibly three on a Saturday and another three on Sunday.

My program had two elite teams in middle school. I estimate that one of our teams, alone, played in sixteen tournaments per year, which is approximately 96 games per season. That is more games than are in an NBA season. That number is also triple the number of games that college or high school teams play. This type of schedule is not only intense, but it does not leave much room for training. It can also play a role in poor academic performance as well as injuries.

I remember winning the championship at the MIT tournament in Maryland in 2019. The game started at around 6pm; after winning the tournament, it was probably around 8pm when we hit the road to go home.

After the four-and-a-half-hour drive, we dropped the boys off or put them in an Uber, and we returned the rental van. I got home around 2am. All of this and our players had to get to school the next day with tired and sore bodies. This was not a healthy situation when you consider the effect such a trip may have had on their attention span in class the next day. As their coach, I was complicit in that mental and physical wear and tear.

I call this the basketball matrix. It is out of control, and we all are guilty of playing a part in it. We are all victims as well. The parents, coaches, players, referees, commissioners—all play a role in this, we are all liable. For example, as a coach, I may have a set schedule for the year and, suddenly, a tournament pops up on the same weekend that previously was an off week for training or practice. Then I might hear through the grapevine that one of our players was going away to a tournament with another team since we were not.

A typical domino effect of events would occur where once one key kid defected other boys would follow. Loyalty is a curse word in the AAU world. As a coach in grassroots basketball, I have also been backed into a corner and have abandoned my schedule to take the team to a tournament just to avoid my players going away with an opposing team.

I have also taken the other route and chosen not to go to a tournament, only to be left in a gym running workouts with only a few kids. This would leave me with an empty feeling in my stomach, fearing that I might not get my players back after they left with another program. This is the inner conflict that most coaches will face in the grassroots basketball world, especially if you are running a program without a sneaker deal as I did for so long.

What about the parents' complicity? Parents, like coaches, must prioritize what is best for their children. Are you going to be the parent that puts playing ahead of training and academics? The pressure comes from many directions. Your child will not know how to say no most times; however, at some point, he or she must be taught the power of the word "no." For most children, playing is a priority, so they will most times put playing above everything else.

When I coached, I wanted my players to remain loyal to the agenda we prescribed for them. If the opposing coach wanted to use a particular weekend to make a play for a child, he would say he "just wants him for this particular tournament." However, that is what I call "tricknology." He might go behind the coach's or parent's back and sell your son a "bag of goods," which includes a sweat suit, a pair of sneakers, free entry into a national camp, and so on. Trust me, I know because I have done the same things. It is part of the behind-the- scenes chess game that is played in grassroots basketball. Again, I am giving you "FREE GAME" on how the business operates at times.

The commissioner of an AAU basketball tournament is like a concert promoter who wants to bring to a venue the best performers, rappers, singers, and groups. Once he signs the attractive headliners, the lesser-known talents will follow, as will the fans. A great commissioner can attract the best teams, starting from the eight-year-old and under division, all the way up to the high school level.

Quality programs lure weaker teams to tournaments to measure their skill level and talent. Most times, they serve as bait in the early bracket games of tournaments to reel in the bigger fish. The commissioner's main objective is money while running a quality event. He can get money from admission fees from fans and parents, sponsorships, and concessions. If a commissioner gets twelve teams per division at $350.00 per team, $4,200 overall, that can result in a great financial come up, or as we say in the culture, a big bag! I can go on and on about the different agendas in grassroots basketball.

PLAYER WELL-BEING

What really gets lost in this basketball matrix is the well-being of the children. Quite frankly, children are playing too many games. In his article, "These kids are ticking time bombs: the threat of youth basketball," Baxster Holmes, ESPN Senior writer, quotes Tim DiFrancesco, the Los Angeles Lakers' head strength and conditioning coach: "parts of it are excellent. But also, parts of it are very broken, especially as it relates to injuries in the league (NBA). What we're seeing is a rash of injuries among young players."

NBA commissioner Adam Silver has noticed a trend also: "what our orthopedics are telling us, is they're seeing wear-and-tear issues in young players that they didn't used to see until players were much older." When speaking on the same topic, Chris Powers, a USC professor and the director of its biokinesiology program, stated, "We see kids all the time that are 10, 11 years old with really bad tendinitis and overuse injuries all the time. I've seen ACL tears in 11-years-olds."

As a coach on the front lines, I realize our children do not know how to stretch properly, get rest, or allow their bodies to recover. So, yes, the basketball matrix is hurting the game; we all need to become more disciplined when it comes to the amount of playing and training we expect of our children. As Sebastian Telfair and his circle taught me, it is very important to know the value of our youth as it pertains to their bodies. As the saying goes: use basketball, don't let it use you!

THE FUNDAMENTALS: IMPORTANCE

I live by the motto "No guts, No glory." Training is a key part of the game. You cannot dodge the sweat and work it takes to get better and you need to be honest with your approach. To improve in anything, you must dedicate yourself to the gym or, what we in the basketball world call, "The Lab." You should be putting up 500 shots per day minimum if you are in high school. You have to do the boring work of shooting 500 free throws per day. Do not train for Instagram likes. Your mixtapes or workout videos might be nice, but the real work is done when no one is watching. Fundamentals cannot be ignored, no matter how boring the repetition can be at times. The earlier you teach your child how to use both their right hand and their left hands efficiently the better. Time must be spent on shooting the ball with proper form.

Practice is important, but so is safety. If you are teaching a child between the ages of eight and twelve, you should not use a regulation ball, which can be too heavy for them. Regulation size basketballs can throw off a child's mechanics. It can corrupt their shooting form for their entire lives. It is important to make running, jumping jacks, and jumping rope a part of their daily routine by the time they are ten years old.

Lately, grassroots basketball has seen a surge of people enter the game as "trainers." While some of them know what they are doing—and I know some great trainers—many are doing drills with kids that will never translate to a game. I have seen trainers put players through drills as if they are getting players ready for a circus rather than a basketball game. As Dr. Rob Newton stated,

"Many athlete coaches and strength/conditioning specialists are adopting fads and fallacies which have little or no scientific basis as they try to gain some competitive edge or demonstrate that they are doing things which are new or different. Often these novel products, training systems and philosophies are driven purely by commercial interests."

Even Deion Sanders, who is now the head football coach at Jackson State University, expressed his disappointment on Twitter concerning what he called, "circus" trainers. "Athletes, please stop doing all these crazy drills that don't apply to your game. A trainer or coach should be able to show how this translates to your game. If he or she can't, stop the madness now."

Over the past few years, I have noticed a rash of children who play like robots and lack instincts. Often, they lack a feel for the game and play with more of a textbook approach. When I grew up, we played three-on-three and four-on-four in the park. That style of play taught us early how to use a pick and roll, how to move without the ball, and how to learn and read angles. On defense, there was no hiding. You had to keep your man in front of you and provide help when needed to stop ball penetration. The Olympics recently added three-on-three basketball to their vast competition field. "The genesis of FIBA wanting to get three-on-three in the Olympics was to give a wider range of basketball players a chance to become Olympians," said Stu Jackson, NBA TV analyst and former NBA executive.

Matt Santangelo, a former Gonzaga University guard, is the executive director of Hoopfest. It is the largest three-on-three basketball tournament in the world and takes place each summer in Spokane, Washington. He stated: "Each player in 3-on-3 needs to have a hybrid skill set, because everyone has to do everything—score, rebound and pass." It is no wonder we used the three-on-three and four-on-four games in our Brooklyn Nets pre-draft workouts, especially when we wanted to analyze a player's basketball IQ and decision-making ability on the court. I believe learning the game through three-on-three, and four-on-four competition gave me a better understanding of basketball.

When I scouted, I used to marvel at the number of prospects who made it to the big stage on pure athleticism or natural talent. They were able to hide their lack of fundamentals. I've scouted college guards who could dominate their position simply based on their physical prowess. For example, "power guards" were usually able to get where they wanted on the court. One player, in particular, got to the college level with big-time accolades largely because of his strength. However, his stock dropped precipitously in his freshman year due to lack of a jump shot. His mechanics were bad and he shot a "hard ball." He never made it to the NBA after being a high school All-American.

I once scouted a wing from a big-time school who could jump over everyone on the court. However, he could not put the ball on the floor to create his own shot and his shooting range was limited. Again, his stock dropped, and he did not get drafted, despite having a big name in college.

I think about the big man I evaluated, who lacked post skills and proper footwork and could not score against defenders his own size. Somewhere along the line he was cheated out of learning the basics needed at the highest levels of basketball. *Did he pass up on training to play in more games? Did he lack the discipline needed to work on his skill set?* These are the questions I often asked myself when I dropped players in my personal rankings. I know a lot of my peers from other NBA teams did the same.

CONDITIONING

Recently, there have been drastic cuts in physical education funding in America. "In many states across the country, schools allow exemptions and waivers from physical education classes, and funding for PE averages a mere $764 per school, per year, according to a 2016 survey from the Society of Health and Physical Educators."

More often than not, children who come to my practices cannot run a few laps without huffing and puffing. Due to this lack of conditioning, I have often had to impose rigorous strength and conditioning tactics into both my AAU and high school programs.

An athlete's conditioning should start off as a general approach to getting in shape and getting stronger. It is commonly advised to start intense training when the athlete is twelve or thirteen years old. I participate often in the training with my players. I take them to the park where we run steps together. I also do calisthenics with my team, consisting of pull-ups, push-ups, arm dips, and more. I see it as a form of bonding to run laps with my players. We motivate each other to be our best selves.

Early on as a scout, I sat in on New Jersey Nets practices, where I witnessed former head coach Lawrence Frank's method of bonding with his players. Every time his team of multimillionaires ran full court sprints during the practice, he ran as well. I was very impressed.

He was pushing his players to get in better shape with sprints, while contributing to the overall morale of his team.

Years later, when Coach Kenny Atkinson was the head coach of the Brooklyn Nets, I noticed that he and his coaches stayed in great shape with a work ethic that was second to none. During practices they were able to demonstrate plays at full speed. They also consistently worked out with the players. After practices, their shirts would be just as drenched with sweat as those of the Nets' players.

At Bishop Loughlin, I incorporated conditioning into our pre-season culture and utilized the outdoor track. I required my guards to run a 5:30 mile. It was mandatory for my bigs, or players six-feet-three or taller, to run a 6:00 mile.

When eventual McDonald's All-American and Villanova University stand out, six-feet-five JayVaughn Pinkston was a freshman at Bishop Loughlin, he ran steps during our first scrimmage game. He was punished for not qualifying for his mile run the first time; eventually, he made it after a couple of attempts. His play on the court improved as his strength and conditioning got better. He was not unique; he was just an example of a player I pushed to get better by putting an emphasis on conditioning. It is a critical component of sports that too often is ignored early in an athlete's career. However, it is likely the most important factor in having stamina and longevity in the game.

I am a believer in children doing exercises as early as eight years old. I am especially a big proponent of workouts that involve natural body weight which, for young children, includes push-ups and sit-ups. Children can also sprint and jog to start, which aids in building up their lungs and endurance. According to *Healthfully*, written by Kathy Gleason, "It's important to get children active as early as possible because kids who exercise when they are young are more likely to stick with that good habit as adults." I totally agree that the earlier children are introduced to exercise, the better, and that planting those early seeds in the mindset of children is key to a healthy lifestyle. And, since one in three children is obese, all youth should follow a similar regimen.

Former First Lady Michelle Obama deserves a lot of credit for using her platform to address obesity issues in children with her "Let's Move!" agenda. "It's about learning about all the different ways to eat healthy and to strike those balances and to be active— whether that means playing a sport, which many kids do," she said. "But not every kid is an athlete, and they don't have to be ... because you can get the exercise you need from walking your dog vigorously, running with your dog, doing some push-ups at home or just playing."

Young ladies, in particular, benefit big time from being active. The more they are engaged in physical activity, the more resilient they may be to some of the pressures society places on them. In gymnastics, young children are known to start training as early as kindergarten. Some children start national training sessions when they are ten years old.

> "From the time she's a toddler, a girl is bombarded with media and other cultural messages that undermine the kind of healthy, resilient self-image you want her to develop. But parents have a tremendous influence on how a girl feels about herself, and with the right map in hand, you can steer your daughter away from influences and activities that undermine self-esteem and towards those that contribute to a realistic body image and a strong sense of self."
> —Juliann Garey, "Raising Girls with Healthy Self-Esteem," Child Mind Institute

It has been a blessing to witness the benefits that exercising and working out have done for some of the young ladies in my program. I have witnessed girls who hated to simply run or jog. The science of movement and running helped remove their "security blankets."

When they dug deep, it woke them up to a mental toughness they probably were not aware existed. That intrinsic edge can carry them through life when they are faced with adversity.

It has been a great joy to see stars, such as Olympic gymnast Dominique Dawes and Olympic figure skater Michelle Kwan, use their platforms to advocate for young girls to be active in fitness and sports. I was also inspired by the late Kobe Bryant's desire to champion girls' basketball, as he supported his late daughter Gianna's basketball career. Bryant said his Mamba Academy was "a natural expansion of my commitment to educating and empowering the next generation of kids through sports." Bryant was also very visible and outspoken in his support of the WNBA. He often attended LA Sparks' games when his former teammate, Derek Fisher, was the coach. Overall, it is very important for both boys and girls in sports to be more conscious of their health and nutrition. For the young athlete, health is indeed wealth!

CHAPTER 14

SELF-MANAGEMENT, SELF-CARE, VIDEO GAMES

Video games have become overwhelmingly present in many homes all over the globe. When I coached in the summer of 2018, the video game Fortnight Battle Royale was the most popular game internationally. Epic Games reportedly garnered three billion dollars in profits from it. I have observed the more video games children are playing, the less they are playing outside. In many instances, video games take away from our children's innate ability to create.

According to the market research firm Childwise, "Children aged five to sixteen spend an average of six and a half hours a day in front of a screen compared with around three hours in 1995. Teenaged boys spend the longest, with an average of eight hours. Eight-year-old girls spend the least—three-and-a-half hours."

Screen time is described as "time spent watching TV, playing game consoles, or using a mobile device, computer or tablet." When I grew up, video games were a minimal factor in households. Of course, Atari and Pacman are no match for today's PlayStation 5 Pro or Xbox One X 1TB. Instead of sitting in front of a screen, I was outside playing basketball, stick ball, touch and tackle football, shooting dice, racing against the homies on the block, and playing Manhunt. Okay, I'm done reminiscing, but you get the point.

Recently, I have noticed that the overindulgence in video games by children I have coached has led to sleep deprivation. According to a *Washington Parent* article by Cheryl Maguire, "artificial blue light is emitted from electronic screens. This type of light causes the brain to suppress the hormone melatonin which your body needs to sleep." Research by the American Academy of Sleep Medicine found "gamers who played for seven hours or more experienced both poor and less sleep than non-gamers."

According to the National Heart, Lung and Blood Institute, school-age children and teens should sleep nine to ten hours per night. Sleep disruptions or lack of the proper amount of sleep increases the risk of obesity, heart disease, stroke, and diabetes. The proper amount of sleep promotes growth and development, improves social interactions, and increases immunity against diseases.

So, if you are going to be in an AAU tournament, you need as much sleep as possible. When our ninth grade New Heights/Lightning team participated in the Nike EYBL (Elite Youth Basketball League) tournament in the summer of 2021, the coaching staff and I noticed that when we had morning games, (before 11:30am), players usually started games sluggishly. When we asked our boys what seemed to be the problem, almost all of them admitted that they were not getting a lot of sleep at night due to video games, watching television, or just talking all night with one another.

Parents and coaches, I recommend that you do not let your children/players take video games on the road and, sometimes, it is necessary to take their phones to keep them off social media at night. If your best player is up past midnight when you have a game the next morning at nine, you could be heading for a complete disaster! I am not suggesting that parents forbid their children from playing video games—that would be unrealistic. However, I am suggesting that parents at least limit the number of hours a child spends playing them.

Like in anything else, balance is the key. Instead of video games, have your child read a book, which leads to enhanced critical thinking. Black and brown children, especially, need to spend more time reading and exploring the world through books. It will only help their reading comprehension, which is a key factor in success of the standardized tests that eventually they will have to take.

TIME MANAGEMENT: DISTRACTIONS AND SACRIFICES

Any athlete must know that the more success they have, the more distractions they will encounter. Interruptions like the googly eyes a girl gives you after previously looking the other way. Or disturbances like your homies wanting you to hang out at the mall when you need to be studying for an exam or putting up shots in the gym.

Distractions now come in the form of the lure of getting on a video game late at night, even though you have two or three AAU games in the morning. Or, from social media, sitting for hour after hour obsessively watching your followers or likes go up or down. Distractions are the direct messages sent back and forth when arguing with a troll, or an excessive amount of time spent on TikTok or YouTube, looking at new music videos or other things of interest.

Ultimately, distractions will always exist. As time progresses, they will reinvent themselves. You can help your child sift through the maze and stay focused by teaching him/her the discipline of time management. Teach them early to prioritize what is most important. Kobe Bryant referred to these types of sacrifices in his book, *Mamba Mentality*. Kobe stated he sacrificed his sleep to be successful, going to the gym early, before his wife and kids woke up, and going to the gym late after his wife and kids were already in bed.

What are you willing to sacrifice for your children to get better? How will you help them feed their hunger for the game they love? The parent who has a child between the ages of seven and twelve must set a good example with time management skills. The younger the age group, the more they must rely on parents to help them travel to practice and games. Time management starts with a mindset. I have seen parents from Long Island travel an hour and a half both ways to every game and practice in Brooklyn, while rarely showing up late. On the other hand, I have witnessed parents and children that live twenty minutes away rarely arriving on time to practice or games.

In my parent meetings as an AAU director, I always made sure I highlighted and emphasized the amount of time that must be dedicated to their child's development. It is as simple as this: if you are a partier, you will probably need to cut down on your extracurricular activities on Friday night. It is not fun to wake up with a hangover when you have to go from gym to gym in the middle of the July heat. Your child's whole weekend can easily be consumed by a tournament. You might be sleeping and eating in the car between games. You will be driving up and down the highways, for hours sometimes, to get to tournaments. Your Saturday can easily start at seven in the morning or earlier and end twelve hours later.

What a commitment you need to make as a parent! If you have other children, then you are also juggling other wants and needs. The whole lifestyle can be extremely stressful. Be ready to ask a family member for help. Remember the African proverb, "It takes a village to raise a child." Hopefully, your coach or another parent can help with transportation when you can't get to a game. "Where there is a will there is a way...." Your child's success will depend on that.

THE AGE OF CORONA

As I complete this book, I am writing in the midst of the COVID-19 pandemic in New York City, the epicenter of the crisis. Former New York City mayor, Bill de Blasio, did not issue summer permits for the local parks for 2020. Therefore, the New York City tradition of youth summer tournaments were non-existent because of social distancing mandates. Both fall/winter indoor high school sports in New York City, and in many other cities in the U.S., were suspended.

Parents, students, and teachers had to struggle with remote learning for a whole year. Most of us missed the social interactions of being in classrooms, gyms, and locker rooms.

All these developments served as more assaults on my community, thanks to an invisible entity that has had no mercy. The Coronavirus represents a new reality for so many industries. Youth sports generated more than $18 billion, annually, before the pandemic. My Brooklyn Bridge Basketball program certainly contributed to a small portion of that, thanks to all the traveling and playing we have done over the years.

In the summer of 2020, we were scheduled to travel to the Under Armor future circuit, as well as to the AAU Nationals. But we had to abandon all our spring and summer events. Yep, our season was cancelled just like the NCAA's March Madness. Further, the NBA season of 2020 was postponed before the league formed their "bubble" in Orlando, Florida.

In the past, we enrolled our youth teams in numerous summer tournaments all around the city. Those tournaments often ran from nine in the morning until six or seven in the evening, depending on the age group. For the first time that I could remember, there was a void in the summer basketball world, like a crater left in the earth by a falling comet or space debris.

The unknown is scary. So much is at stake, going forward. Sports programs and venues will surely update new policies to guard against the transmission of the Coronavirus and other viruses, and there may be potential lawsuits. There will be new common sense risk management policies in place. For example, at the 2021 EYBL tournament in Augusta, Georgia, all players and coaches had to get tested for Coronavirus almost daily. Many universities are mandating that their students get the vaccine. Crowd sizes have decreased. There are often daily temperature checks of all staff and players involved with sporting events. Hand sanitizers and Lysol are as readily available as towels and water bottles used to be. Traditional water fountains could be as ancient as phone booths. Sporting equipment will likely no longer be shared amongst teammates.

Recently, it was announced that New York City will no longer have remote learning in the fall of 2021, which means athletic competition should go back to normal. However, in the New York City Public School Athletic League (PSAL), all children must be vaccinated to participate. Meanwhile, the Catholic league, while not mandating their athletes get the vaccine, is requiring that children play sports with masks on.

While the NBA is not mandating that players get the COVID-19 vaccine, local vaccination requirements in such cities as New York and San Francisco prohibit players from competing or practicing in home arenas without proof of at least one vaccine dose. Superstar Kyrie Irving of the Brooklyn Nets was at first allowed to play only in away arenas. He was unvaccinated and, originally, could not play in his home Barclays arena due to the NYC vaccine mandate. The mandate has since been lifted by the city's current mayor, Eric Adams.

Aaron Rodgers, star quarterback of the Green Bay Packers, tested positive for COVID in the 2021 season, after stating he was "immunized" when asked by a reporter if he was vaccinated. He was held from competition until he tested negative again. Recently, Washington State head coach Nick Rolovich was fired from his position for not complying with the statewide vaccine mandate. Again, this pandemic has turned the world as we once knew it upside down, and the sports world is a mere microcosm of this new dynamic.

MENTAL HEALTH

In my nine years as an NBA scout, I participated in interviews that left my colleagues and me in awe. I wondered often how some of these young men made it through childhood after dealing with so much trauma. Yet there they were, in a room full of decision-makers, so close to being drafted by an NBA team.

I traveled all over the country following prospects that I thought would be great fits for the Nets organization. Yet, many times a player was "red flagged" by our team psychiatrist for personal problems that the doctor determined were insurmountable. Frequently, I found it unfortunate that a young brother who had been blessed with so many physical gifts would fall short of his ultimate goal due to an untreated mind.

In the past, mental health disorders such as depression and anxiety were considered stigmas in this country. However, according to the American Psychological Association Survey, Americans are becoming more open about mental health: "a total of 87 percent of American adults agreed that having a mental health disorder is nothing to be ashamed of, and 86 percent said they believe that people with mental health disorders can get better."

However, the same article cites "young adults between eighteen and 34 reported the poorest mental health of those surveyed, as well as the most shame around mental health disorders." The article goes on to say, "young adults were also more likely than older age groups to believe that most mental health disorders do not require treatment." I can relate to this sentiment because, as a young adult, my mother advised me to go into treatment, but I resisted. I did not see the need to talk to someone I did not know about my issues. I thought a therapist was a waste of my time and was simply a mind hustler. I wanted no parts of it. I certainly was in denial and, as a young adult, I preferred to take my issues to a bottle of alcohol or a bag of weed. I was wrong. Therapy was once taboo, and it is certainly stigmatized in black and brown communities.

According to the U.S. Department of Health and Human Services Office of Minority Services, African Americans are twenty percent more likely to experience serious psychological distress, such as major depression, suicide, PTSD, and anxiety, than are non-Hispanic whites. The Mayo Clinic defines Post-Traumatic Stress Disorder (PTSD) as a mental health condition that is triggered by a terrifying event—either experiencing it or witnessing it. Symptoms may include flashbacks, nightmares, and severe anxiety, as well as uncontrollable thoughts about the event.

Other listed symptoms that stood out to me as it pertains to my community include:

- Negative thoughts about yourself, other people or the world
- Hopelessness about the future
- Feeling emotionally numb
- Always being on guard for danger
- Self-destructive behavior, such as drinking too much or driving too fast
- Trouble sleeping
- Trouble concentrating
- Irritability, angry outbursts or aggressive behavior
- Overwhelming guilt or shame

To be very blunt, the black community in this country has been subjected to trauma that is unmatched in the world. It is estimated that at least six million Africans— ten to fifteen percent—died during the infamous "Middle Passage" across the Atlantic Ocean during the more than 300 years of the Transatlantic Slave Trade. Our people were classified in the American Constitution as three-fifths human and were treated worse than some animals.

The Three-Fifths Compromise of 1787 was a political move by the House of Representatives of that era to give Southern states more representation and more electoral votes. Overall, this was a strategic game used by racists. My ancestors were the property of slave owners who worked them from "can't see in the morning to can't see at night." They served ruthless men and women who left thick lashes on the backs of our forefathers and viciously raped our mothers. Black women gave birth to babies who were sold to different plantations or forced labor camps never to be seen again.

Black Codes, enacted after the American Civil War from 1865-1866, enforced laws to prohibit blacks from holding any occupation other than farmer or servant, unless they paid an annual tax of $10 to $100. The Black Codes featured degrading laws such as making black people stick their heads in "laughing barrels" to prohibit them from laughing in the presence of white people. Or, moving to the street when white people walked on the same sidewalk, since it was illegal to share the same space with a white person.

The generational trauma changed its formula during the Red Summer, or mass white race terrorism of 1919, where black men were hung from trees, often castrated, and burned at the stake. Black towns and communities were burned to the ground by those who were jealous of black success and excellence. White people used to make the lynching of black people a regional event, as entire families—yes, men, women, and children—would come from near and far to celebrate and watch. Body parts were saved as souvenirs and pictures of the hanging brother or sister were placed on postcards. The Ku Klux Klan, alone, was said to be responsible for 64 lynchings in 1918 and 83 in 1919, according to Red Summer of 1919.

> *Southern trees bear a strange fruit*
> *Blood on the leaves and blood at the root*
> *Black bodies swinging in the southern breeze*
> *Strange fruit hanging from the poplar trees*
> *—Billie Holiday*

> *"Indeed, in America there is a strange and powerful belief that if you stab a black person ten times, the bleeding*

*stops, and the healing begins the moment the assailant
drops the knife."*
—Ta-Nehisi Coates

All that history only touches on a small fraction of black people's collective trauma. In modern times, black people are still terrorized by the lynchings we have witnessed via technology. How many times have we watched the suffocation of Eric Garner while he pled, "I can't breathe"? We watched George Floyd in Minnesota repeat "I can't breathe" while a police officer pressed his knee on his neck for more than nine minutes. Or, the video of Walter Scott, who ran from police before being gunned down in the back in South Carolina. Or, Rayshard Brooks who was gunned down in similar fashion by police in Atlanta.

Years before all these atrocities, and like so many other people, I watched Rodney King suffer a fifteen-minute beating on video by four police officers. Ultimately, he suffered from permanent brain damage, a broken right leg, cuts and bruises on his body, and a burn on his chest when he was jolted with a 50,000-volt stun gun. I was only eleven years old when I marched with my father in the Bronx to protest the untimely death of Eleanor Bumpers, the 66-year-old black woman who was killed by two shots from a white policeman's twelve-gauge shotgun.

Yusuf Hawkins's death is still deeply embedded in my psyche. He was born the same year as I was—1973— however, he would only live to be sixteen years old. He was chased by a white mob of white youth with bats in the Bensonhurst section of Brooklyn. One of them murdered Yusef by shooting him in the chest. Yusef was in that neighborhood simply to buy a car.

Along with their own personal traumas, our biggest sports heroes have had to endure mental trauma due to the racism that has spread as fast as any germ that ever existed. Jack Johnson was the first black heavyweight boxing champion in the world. He held that title from 1908-1915, beating up both white and black opponents. A black man holding the heavyweight title was a significant blow to the symbolism of white supremacy in America, the standard bearer for racism in the world.

Johnson's biggest crime against white society was not beating up white men in the ring, but rather his assault on the white male ego. Whites did not like the way Johnson flaunted his wealth and ran around town with white women. This was bold and brash behavior for any black man in 1908. Soon, he would face trumped up charges of transporting a prostitute across state lines. After skipping bail, he lived abroad for seven years before turning himself in and spending almost a year in jail. How did Johnson deal with his fall from grace? How did he cope with being in jail after being the champ? What went into his psyche that made him feel like a white woman was just as much of a trophy as his heavyweight belt?

Johnson described himself as suicidal at times, "I would have killed myself by leaping from a window of a hotel in Portland, Me., a year ago (after defending the heavyweight title). My wife stayed up nights nursing me. As a result, she became a nervous wreck," according to Charles Johnson's article in The Chicago Tribune. Later, Johnson's wife would commit suicide.

How much torture did Jesse Owens have to endure when competing in the Berlin Olympics in front of Adolph Hitler and his Nazi party? Hitler refused to take a picture with Jesse because he did not want to acknowledge that a black man was more of a superior athlete than someone of the Aryan race.

More egregious than Hitler's was the treatment Owens received from his own U.S. President, Franklin D. Roosevelt. Owens stated, "Hitler didn't snub me—it was [Roosevelt] who snubbed me. The president didn't even send me a telegram." On top of that, Roosevelt only invited white Olympians to the White House in 1936. How do you think Jesse coped with being shunned? Can you imagine how it felt to win four gold medals at the Olympics in a fascist country only to be disrespected in your home, the native country for which you competed, the so-called "land of the free and home of the brave?" What sense of betrayal did Owens feel? In his later years, Jesse raced against horses and dogs, just to stay out of poverty. How much resentment did Owens have? How did he deal with it?

Branch Rickey, the sports executive of the Brooklyn Dodgers, reportedly chose Jackie Robinson to be the first black person to play in a Major League Baseball game due to his baseball talent, but also because of his temperament. Rickey needed someone who was not going to strike back against all the slurs and insults that would confront Robinson for the majority of his career. How much emotion did he have to suppress when offended? Did he displace his anger in other ways? How did his family cope with him being consistently disrespected in public?

Africatown is three miles north of downtown Mobile, Alabama. It was the home of the last "known" illegal slave ship to land in America, which arrived 52 years after the slave trade was abolished. When slaves became free, they built stores, farms, schools, and raised their families in Africatown. Over the years, they even produced a few notable athletes, including baseball legend Hank Aaron.

During the 1973-74 Major League Baseball season, as Aaron chased Babe Ruth's homerun record, he was sent an abundance of hate mail and his life was threatened continually. The atmosphere was so intense that his family had to be protected by armed guards. Even when he retired, he was forced to miss his children's graduations. His children also had to have police escorts at school, due to the envy and hate generated by their father's dominance in a sport. What kind of trauma did that cause him and his family? What kind of anxieties did Aaron deal with when he was receiving hate mail? Did he become paranoid when he was threatened? What scars were left on his psyche and on that of his family members'?

Where do black people go to treat their anger, rage, and feelings of hopelessness? How do we deal with our numbness? How do we cope internally when we have to "go along just to get along," in a country where we are not respected? Quite honestly, it is the reason why we self-medicate often with destructive treatments such as drugs and alcohol.

Traditionally, barbershops and beauty parlors in the hood have been places where we vent our frustrations. On numerous occasions, I have had deep conversations with brothers from my community when getting a haircut. We have discussed everything from racism to hip hop, relationships, sex, sports, politics and more. But, for our collective trauma, fear, depression, anger, and frustration, the barbershop or the beauty parlor is certainly not enough!

> "To be a Negro in this country and to be relatively
> conscious is to be in a rage almost all the time."
> —James Baldwin.

> "I take a blunt to take the pain out, if I wasn't high, I'd
> probably blow my brain out."
> —2pac

> Watch me put my heart in this cup
> In my feelings
> She's my therapist
> I'm going to talk to this cup
> —Moneybagg Yo

As a coach who has always been in the trenches with my players, I have certainly dealt with youth who are coping with mental horrors. One of the eight-and-under boys in my program saw his father gunned down on a street corner when he was only six years old. Another player witnessed his mother murdered in the very apartment where he still resides to this day. A young brother who played for me witnessed his mother on drugs most of his young life; she died earlier than she should. At the time of this writing, I lost one of my former players from a stabbing near a Bed Stuy park. Also, the father of one of my players recently died of cancer on his son's birthday. The father had only been back in the home for a year after a stint in prison. These are just some of the stories that are personal to me; however, there are many of these narratives in every hood.

What kind of PTSD do these children have? How much have they suffered socially from being in and out of school due to remote learning and COVID restrictions during this COVID era?

"Kids that experience things like domestic violence, gun violence, and child abuse become teenagers and young adults with PTSD symptoms. Only about one-quarter of African Americans seek mental health care, compared to 40% of whites. Not getting treatment and learning to manage PTSD can turn to depression, bipolar disorder, or other personality disorders. Many times, this can lead to some type of conflict with the criminal justice system, which can begin a whole new cycle of issues. PTSD is one of the more common psychiatric disorders in youth detention facilities, with the probability of PTSD being at least 1 in 10 detained youth."[32]

If you are a coach, the likelihood is that at least one person on your team is suffering from untreated mental illness. Therefore, it is more than worth it to have our children treated sooner rather than later. LeBron James, Kevin Love and Michael Phelps all deserve a lot of credit for using their platforms to take the stigma out of mental illness. Counseling and trauma therapy are already major parts of the I PROMISE School curriculum that Lebron created.

Love discussed his anxiety issues courageously in an open letter he wrote in the Player's Tribune. "For 29 years, I thought about mental health as someone else's problem," he wrote. "To me, it was

---

[32] Contributors. "PTSD is more common than you think." *Black Youth Project*. 22 May 2018.

a form of weakness that could derail my success in sports or make me seem weird or different." Love credits therapy for his growth. "I think it's easy to assume we know ourselves, but once you peel back the layers it's amazing how much there is to still discover," he said.

Recently, Naomi Osaka, the number two women's tennis player, withdrew from the French Open and from Wimbledon, stating she suffered from both anxiety and depression. Gymnastic superstar Simone Biles withdrew from the 2021 summer Olympics in Tokyo. She stated that her "mind, body and soul are simply not in sync." As these famous athletes keep leading the way with their voices, it will make the topic more comfortable. Our children deserve a chance, and it starts with addressing what has been hurting them mentally. There are many free opportunities to get your children treated for their mental health. Seek out the help, our babies deserve it!

As I conclude this book, I hope my passion and love touches the parents and children it was meant to serve. My ultimate goal is to address the youth sports industry from a black perspective and get to the root of key issues that have been brought to my attention. I want black/brown parents and children not only to know some of the obstacles that they will face, but to be informed about how to navigate their particular journey.

Free Game is a manual that you can use from the start to the finish of your marathon run in the sports world. In the spirit of coaching, I attempted to motivate, inspire, lead, and hold accountable both parents and children to excel both on and off the court or playing fields. Again, while my background is heavily based in the basketball world, I am confident that parents and children in track and field, soccer, baseball, football, and other sports can take "jewels" from *Free Game* and use them for their specific sport. I am honored that you have taken the time to read it.

THE MECCA... I THANK YOU...

Mecca is the holiest city in the Islamic faith. It is the birthplace of Prophet Muhammad (peace and blessings be upon him) and it is also the city that Muslims are required to visit at least one time in their lifetime in a pilgrimage known as the Hajj. New York City is called The Mecca of basketball because, here, "the game" is a religion. The holy grounds the games are played on are Dyckman, Gersh Park, West 4th Street, Hoops in the Sun, IS8, Tillary Park, Conrad McRae and Fun Sport, to name a few. The symbolic Imams or Ministers of these parks are the commissioners who lead their congregations or their teams, parents, and staff to the promised land safely.

These brothers and sisters who lead these tournaments do it from the heart. They set up the scoreboards early in the morning and deal with schedule changes on the fly. They play the role of meteorologists and check the clouds early in the morning, praying that games don't get rained out. They employ some of our most vulnerable youth with summer jobs to sell water and Gatorade to thirsty parents watching their children play.

The Kaaba is an ancient black stone located inside the Grand Mosque in the holy city of Mecca. Muslims performing the Hajj circle the Kaaba seven times. It serves as a focal and unifying point. Harlem's 155th Street is where the legendary Holcombe Rucker Park is located. In New York, the Rucker serves as a unifying point where so many basketball greats knew they had to touch down and pay homage to the soil. NBA greats Wilt Chamberlain, Dr. J, Kareem Abdul Jabbar, Connie Hawkins, Chris Mullin, Allen Iverson, Kevin Garnett, and Kobe Bryant all left their sweat there. So did street legends Joe Hammond, Earl "the Goat" Manigault, Pee Wee Kirkland, Fly Williams, "Skip to my Lou," Master Rob, Bone Collector, Alimoe, The Future, Kareem Reid, and The Franchise (Rest in Power).

I want to thank Greg Marius, the commissioner and founder of the new Rucker (Rest in Power) who, in 2003, would prove to be more important to the basketball community of NYC than the late NBA commissioner David Stern. In the summer of 2003, hip hop legends Jay-Z and Fat Joe showed that they were the two best sports team owners in the world. Jay Z and his "S. Carter Team" and Fat Joe's "Terror Squad" clashed at the legendary Rucker Park. Both teams would bring out a Who's Who of the basketball world, including Stephon Marbury, Jamal Crawford, Sebastian Telfair, Al Harrington, Jermaine O'Neal, Ron Artest, Lamar Odom and others. They are also responsible for the greatest game that was NEVER played, due to the summer blackout. It was rumored that Jay Z had LeBron James and Shaquille O'Neal on deck to play for free in the hood against The Terror Squad. Whew!

I have love for most of the tournament commissioners in New York City: Rick Rivers, (Funsport), Rudy King (SmartBall), Deon Merritt (Real Skillz), Dame (Gersh), Anton Marchand (Conrad McRae), Rah (Zone 6), George (Pre-Teen) and especially legends like Pete Edwards of IS8, famous for saying, "Bring your game not your name." He put on some of the best events the hood has ever seen.

On April 26th, 2002, 'Tiny' Morton and I brought THE LeBron James to South Jamaica, Queens, to play with Sebastian, after they had completed a joint photo shoot for *Slam* magazine. Our team featured other homegrown Brooklyn Bridge Basketball players such as Karron Clarke (University of Miami), Chris Taft (University of Pittsburgh), and Ramel Bradley (University of Kentucky). We played against Gary Charles and the NY Panthers, which featured local 'killers' Curtis Sumpter and Jason Frazier (Villanova University). The tiny IS8 gym was packed wall to wall, standing room only, an absolute fire hazard. LeBron remembered the game vividly when asked about it. He called the gym, "Hostile. The fans were all over the court." (Armstrong, Kevin. *Daily News*. 10 Jun 2017.)

The official who makes the call for prayer in Islam is called Muezzin. They have the most majestic, melodic voices in the community, singing out loud in the Arabic language, "God is the Greatest!" Our street ball commentators have the best phonetics in the hood. Their names are David Cha-Ching Teele, Jeff "Hannibal" Banks, Joe Pope, Here's Johnny, and Diamond. I thank you for your voices!! You make the players more focused, the fans talk more shit, and the coach's blood pressure go up with each possession. Your sound is the grit of our city. You all make up THE MECCA. I thank all of you for what you do for our youth!

As a mosque in Islam is a Muslim's place of worship, the high schools in New York City have represented the sanctuary, where so many have come to congregate over the years to see some of the giants of their day. I am thankful for such schools as Power Memorial, that saw a scrawny seven-footer, formerly known as Lew Alcindor, before he was known all over the world as Kareem.

Our city is home to over 1,800 public outdoor parks. All of us who participated in this beautiful game have added to the legacy of THE MECCA. It is up to us to share with the next generation the lessons and blessings we gained from this sport.

"Each one Must teach one to Reach one or more."

Every mind that has ever been touched by sports has a story to tell. I just wanted to offer a few of my own, while helping parents and children with their sports journey. I wish all who have read this book: P.E.A.C.E

Positive Energy Always Creates Elevation!!!!

ABOUT THE AUTHOR

Khalid Green has been a fixture in the New York City basketball community since 1996. He was the founder and executive director of Brooklyn Bridge Basketball, Inc., an organization that promoted character-building skills, education and basketball—in that order. The organization's mission was to provide a platform and a "Bridge for boys and girls to fulfill their inner greatness." This vision is reflective of lessons learned from his parents, and southern maternal and paternal grandparents who taught him discipline, integrity and the value of education.

Khalid served as a graduate assistant under head coach Ray Haskins, at Long Island University when they 'punched their tickets' to the NCAA and NIT tournaments. As an assistant coach at Abraham Lincoln High School in 2002, Mr. Green was instrumental in the team winning a PSAL championship with the future thirteenth overall pick in the 2004 draft, Sebastian Telfair. In addition, he was an assistant coach at Bishop Loughlin and Benjamin Banneker High Schools.

During the 2003 year, Khalid was named head varsity coach for Bishop Loughlin High School. During that five-year tenure, he led the program to two CHSAA semi-final appearances and one Brooklyn/Queens Championship. He also built a reputation for developing and attracting elite talent in New York City. At Loughlin, he coached three high school All-Americans: Doron Lamb (University of Kentucky), JayVaughn Pinkston (Villanova University) and Devin Ebanks (University of West Virginia). In 2004 Khalid founded the Right Bounce Top 60 Tournament. Sponsored by Reebok, it was a showcase game for the top sixth through eighth graders in the tri-state area. The game featured future NBA star Lance Stephenson.

Khalid has served as an administrator/coach for the Juice All- Stars with Dwayne "Tiny" Morton. He was also an administrator/coach with the New York Panthers, led by Gary Charles. The 'go-to' person for basketball in Brooklyn, he has been the subject of numerous articles and was twice nominated for the *Daily News* Coach of the Year Award.

Mr. Green served nine years as a scout with the Brooklyn Nets. In that capacity, he traveled the country evaluating, interviewing, and analyzing both college and professional talent. He conducted background checks and generated scouting reports for prospective players, including college hopefuls, free agents, NBA draft picks and trade candidates. He was a member of the strategy team that resulted in player choices for the organization. In his tenth year with the Nets, he worked with the community relations department. Khalid earned a bachelor's degree from Morehouse College, a master's degree from Long Island University, and a sports management degree from Columbia University.

Mr. Green currently serves as a professor at Long Island University where he has taught several courses on evaluating talent in the NBA as well as philosophies of coaching. He is also the community basketball director for New Heights Youth Inc., where he oversees the development of their community basketball initiatives and partnerships. Furthermore, he is the eighth-grade boys national head coach of New Heights as well as an EYBL coach of the New Heights/ Lightning high school program.

He is the co-founder of the Upnext Podcast which can be found on YouTube, Apple and Spotify, as well as on Instagram @Upnextpod and on twitter @UpNext_pod. He is a member of Advancement in Blacks in Sports.

Khalid resides in Brooklyn, New York, where he spends time with his fiancé, Najuma. He enjoys writing, reading, working on his physical fitness, and walking his dog, Assata. Currently, he mentors coaches, parents, and youth from all over the United States and can be contacted at www.Khaleads.com.

TESTIMONIALS

"I've known Khalid since we were kids, and it is because of him that I am now a 'Basketball Mom.' Khalid got my 8-year-old son involved with his youth basketball program in Brooklyn—it was his first real team experience. He was great with all of the kids and parents. I know now, a couple years in, that I'm lucky to have been introduced to this world by Khalid—he not only knows basketball inside and out, but he also shows and proves the importance of setting young people up for success, on and off the court. His book will be a treasure for parents like me and anyone who is working with young people on their basketball journeys."

—Erica Stanley-Dottin

"Khalid Green is overflowing with insight about the volatile state of AAU basketball for Black boys. I was nowhere near the athlete that my son is, so navigating the right path to take in his development as a student athlete is challenging. Who to trust? Who to listen to? Khalid is reliable, trustworthy and shrewd. *Free Game* is like having a mentor/school guidance counselor on call."

—Tyson Toussant, co-founder of Bionic Yarn

"Khalid Green has been a champion in the basketball community in New York City for many years, including his contributions to the most coveted and respected franchises, the New York Knicks and the Brooklyn Nets. I observed him coach my son for a season, and he has truly earned my respect. As a friend for the last 5+ years, Khalid earned my trust by helping me with my transition and navigation from prison through the hurdles society confronted me with early on in my release. He continues that support to the present day. Khalid's book *Free Game* is a must-read and can be applied to the guidance needed for all walks of life on and off the court."

—Karriem "Scooter" Thomas, co-founder and CEO of Da City of Guards

BIBLIOGRAPHY

Adande, J.A. "Black assistant coaches get hurt the most in recruiting scandals." *TheUndefeated.com*. 6 Oct 2017.

Badenhausen, Kurt. "Michael Jordan Has Made Over $1 Billion From Nike – The Biggest Endorsement Bargain in Sports." *Forbes.com*/editors-picks. 3 May 2020.

Bembry, Jerry. "Makur Maker on his decision to attend Howard: 'I want to change the culture.'" *Theundefeated.com*. 9 Jul 2020.

Blackfives.com

Bondy, Stefan. "Decades Later, Riverside Church Basketball Sexual Abuse Survivor Tries to Find Peace." NY *Daily News* 4 Jan. 2020. https://www.nydailynews.com/sports/basketball/ny-richard-holmes-riverside-high-hawks-scandal-lawsuit-20200104-42icisnhvnbr3bxfraeagugxcm-story.html.

Borzello, Jeff. "How reclassification fast-tracks top prospects to college and the NBA," *ESPN.com*. Jul 2018.

Burdick, Jonathan. "Tracing Erie's History of Redlining." *ErieReader.com*. https://www.ErieReader.com/article/tracing-eries-history-of-redlining. 13 Feb 2019.

Chappel, Bill. Penn State Abuse Scandal: A Guide and Timeline. 21 Jun 2012.

"Child development, 13-16-year-olds." *Greatschools.org*. 13 Sep 2010.

Dauster, Rob. "'It's Very Disappointing': The number of black head coaches continues to fall at college hoops' highest level." *Nbcsports.com.* https://collegebasketball.NBCSports.com/2020/03/03/its-very-disappointing-the-number-of-black-head-coaches-continues-to-fall-at-college-hoops-highest-level/. 3 Mar 2020.

"Dr. Umar Johnson Speaks with Roland Martin About ADHD." *News One Now.* 7 Aug 2017.

Flores, Gerald. "Tracy McGrady's First Adidas Contract Will Blow Your Mind. Find Out How Much T-Mac and His People Were Getting Paid." *Solecollector.com.* 16 Apr 2015.

Ford, Donna, Dr. "Don't Rush to Saddle Children with the A.D.H.D Label." *New York Times* Op-Ed. Updated 1 Feb 2016.

Ford, Donna, Dr. Racism and Sexism in Diagnosing ADHD. 13, Oct. 2011.

Garey, Juliann. "Raising Girls with Healthy Self-Esteem." *Child Mind Institute.* https://childmind.org/article/raising-girls-with-healthy-self-esteem/.

Ghianni, Tim. "U.S. spots group moves to protect young athletes from sex abuse." *Reuters.com.* 12 Jun 2012.

Gilleran, Mike. "Reclassification of grade schooler for athletic reasons: Another example of good parenting or just good thinking?" Santa Clara School of Law. May 2014.

Hill, Jemele. "It's Time for Black Athletes to Leave White Colleges." *The Atlantic.* Oct 2019.

Hobson, Willie. "Fund and Games." *The Washington Post.* 18 Mar 2014.

Holmes, Baxter. "These kids are ticking time bombs: The threat of youth basketball." *ESPN.com.* https://www.ESPN.com/nba/story/_/id/27125793/these-kids-ticking-bombs-threat-youth-basketball. 11 Jul 2019.

Huseman, Jessica. "Why Black Parents Are Homeschooling Their Children." *The Atlantic.* 17 Feb 2015.

Infante, John. "Reclassifying 101: Important Info to Consider Before Reclassifying." *Athleticscholarships.net.*

Johnson, Charles. "The Short Sad story of Café-De Champion-Jack Johnson's Mixed-Race Night Club on Chicago's Southside." *The Chicago Tribune.* 25 May 2018.

Johnson, Michelle. "Long-Term Effects of Being Molested as a Child." *Oureverydaylife.com*

Jones, Drew. *Drew News Report.* 4 Jun 2020.

Jonsson, Patrik; Kenworthy, Josh. *The Christian Science Monitor.* Csmonitor.com. 15 Aug 2016.

Jr.NBA.com. Overview & Philosophy. https://jr.nba.com/coaching-overview-philosophy/

Kalbrosky, Bryan. "What is the peak age in the NBA? Probably 27-years-old." *Hoopshype.com.* 31 Dec 2018.

Kasperkevic, Jana. "A tale of two Brooklyns: there's more to my borough than hipsters and coffee." *The Guardian.* 27 August 2014.

Kendi, Ibram X. "Stamped from the Beginning: The definitive history of racist ideas in America." *PublicAffairs.* 2016.

Kilgore, Adam. "Why Was Howard Playing UNLV Anyway? It Wasn't Just College Football as Usual." *The Washington Post.* 8 Sep 2017.

Koba, Mark. "High School Sports Have Turned into Big Business." CNBC.com. Dec 2012.

Kowalski, Kathiann. "Bullying Has Risen in Areas that Support Trump." *Science News for Student Schools*. 30 Jan 2019.

Kunjufu, Jawanza. Developing Positive Self-Images and Discipline in Black Children. Pg. 12. 2000.

Love, Kevin. "Everyone is Going Through Something." The *Player's Tribune*. https://www.theplayerstribune.com/articles/kevin-love-everyone-is-going-through-something. 6 Mar 2018.

Lynch, Matthew. 4 Troubling Truths About Black Boys and the US Educational System. Aug 2015.

Martin, Josh. "Tony Parker Opens Academy for Basketball, Esports, Music and Education in France." *Closeup360.com*. 7 Oct 2009.

McCoy, Mary Kate. "Schools Cut Back Physical Education as Childhood Obesity Remains High. Study: Standardized Testing Pressure Takes Time Away from Physical Education." *Wpr.org*. https://www.wpr.org/schools-cut-back-physical-education-childhood-obesity-remains-high. 26 Mar 2018.

McLean, Trevor. "Why Parents Must Stop Coaching from the Sideline." *Basketballforcoaches.com*. 26 Jul 2018.

McWhorter, John. "Don't Scrap the Test, Help Black Kids Ace It." The *Atlantic*. 9 May 2019.

Morley, Jefferson; Schwarz, Jon. "National Anthem has been tainted with Racism." *TheIntercept.com*. 13 Sep 2016.

"Mr. Lincoln and Negro Equality." *New York Times*. 28 Dec 1860.

Murphy, Jamal. "Black Assistant Coaches Were Scapegoats in the NCAA Recruiting Trials." *TheUndefeated.com*. 15 May 2019.

Musberger, Brent. "Bizarre Protest by Smith, Carlos Tarnishes Medals." *Chicago American Newspaper*. 1968.

Mustain, Gene. "When the crack scourge swept New York City." NY *Daily News*. Aug 2017.

National Basketball Coaches Association. Nbacoaches.com.

National Sexual Violence Resource Center. https://www.nsvrc.org/

Nelson Mandela's Children Fund. 22 Nov 1997.

Nelson, Ryne. "Steve Nash on Nets Coaching Job: 'I Did Skip the Line, Frankly.'" *Slamonline.com*. 10 Sep 2020.

Nightingale, Bob. "MLB's 'Disgusting' Minority Hiring Woes Continue as Job Candidates Shut Out Again." USA *Today*. 4 Dec 2019.

O'Keefe, Michael. "Bob Oliva, Ex-Christ the King basketball coach, pleads guilty to sexual abuse will not go to prison." NY *Daily News*. 5 Apr 2011.

Perkins, Briley. "The '92 Dream Team: The Team That Changed the Game of Basketball Forever." STMU *History Media*. Oct 2019.

Persico, Claudio. "How Exposure to Pollution Affects Educational Outcomes and Inequality." *Brookings*. 20 Nov 2019.

Prois, Jessica. "Does the SAT Have a Racial Bias." *HuffPost.com*. 25 Apr 2011. Updated 6, Dec 2017.

Psychology.com (positive reinforcement definition).

Public Enemy, "Fear of a Black Planet." "Brothers Gonna Work It Out." Def Jam, Columbia. 1990.

"Redlining: Race and Inequality in America." *Peripherycenter.org.* http://www.peripherycenter.org/culture/redlining-race-inequality. 27 Jan 2015.

"Red Summer of 1919." *History.com.* 26 Jul 2019.

Rhoden, William C. Forty Million Dollar Slaves: The Rise, Fall and Redemption of the Black Athlete. Crown. 11 Jul 2006.

Rhoden, William C. "Where are the Black Coaches in the Power Conferences?" *Theundefeated.com.* 8 Apr 2019.

Robinson, Jackie; Duckett, Alfred. I Never Had It Made: The Autobiography of Jackie Robinson. Ecco Press. 6 May 2003.

Schneider, Jack. "America's Not-So-Broken Education System." *The Atlantic.* Jun 2016.

Siemaszko, Corky; Silva, Daniella; Fieldstadt, Elisha. *NBCnews.com.* 28 Dec 2015.

Simone, Nina. "Nina Simone in Concert." Phillips. 21 Mar, 1 & 6 Apr 1964.

Skiver, Kevin. "Drew Brees Facing Intense Criticism for Comments on Flag Disrespect." *NFL.com.* 3 Jun 2020.

Small, Frank, Ph. D, "Combatting Sexual Abuse in Youth Sports." *Psychology Today.* January 2018

Smith, Michelle. "5 Reasons You want Your Kid to be a Multi-Sport Athlete." *ESPN.com* Oct 2016.

Smith, Stephen A. *First Take.* 3 Sep 2020.

Ssat.com.

Staff Writer. "Adidas Partners with Sebastian Telfair in $15 Million Deal." *Chiefmarketer.com.* 6 May 2004.

Staff Writer. "Tamir Rice Transcript." *Los Angeles Times*. 26 Nov 2014.

"Student." Merriam-Webster Dictionary. 2021.

"Survey: Americans Becoming more open about mental health." American Psychological Association. https://www.apa.org/news/press/releases/2019/05/mental-health-survey. 1 May 2019.

The Katie Couric Interview. *Yahoo Sports*. 4 Nov 2016

Tjarks, Jonathan. "The NBA Draft's Most Polarizing Prospect is a Walking Analytics Experiment." *TheRinger.com*. 27 Nov 2019.

Wertheim, Jon. "Gordon Hayward, the Accidental NBA Star, Is Still Close to His Tennis Roots." *Sports Illustrated*. 28 Sep 2017.

White, Gillian B. "Black Workers Really Do Need to Be Twice as Good." *The Atlantic*. 7 Oct 2015.

Wilbon, Michael. "Mission Impossible: African-Americans & Analytics: Why Blacks are not Feeling the Sports Metrics Movement." *TheUndefeated.com*. https://TheUndefeated.com/features/mission-impossible-african-americans-analytics/. 24 May 2016.

Wilf, Rachel. "Disparities in School Discipline Move Students of Color Toward Prison. New Data Show Youth of Color Disproportionately Suspended and Expelled from School." *Center for American Progress*. 13 Mar 2012.

Whitney Osuigwe Interview. *Sportsstarsoftomorrow.tv*. 17 Mar 2018.

Windhorst, Brian. "Goodbye one and done: With scandals rocking youth basketball NBA readying to step in." *ESPN.com*. 5 Mar 2018.

Zagoria, Adam. "Zion Williamson Signs Multiyear Deal with Jordan Brand." *Forbes.com*/sportsmoney. 23 Jul 2019.

CPSIA information can be obtained
at www.ICGtesting.com
Printed in the USA
JSHW021959281222
35470JS00002B/11

9 781956 019391